We Can Do It!

Roy Larkin

First published in 2013 by

Roy Larkin
PO Box 3066
Reading
RG1 9WP

www.historicroadways.co.uk

© Roy Larkin, 2013

ISBN 978 0 9565014 3 1

Design and typesetting by
Roy Larkin

Printed in England by
Dolman Scott Ltd

Contents

Photographic credits

DB ~ Diane Brazier
FC ~ Fred Cooper
RL ~ Roy Larkin
RLCM ~ Royal Logistic Corps Museum
SR ~ The Scammell Register

Front cover: Scammell Model Y 100-tonner, KD 9168, crossing the Barton swing bridge while en-route from Patricroft to Birkenhead docks. ~ SR

Back cover: 1945 Scammell Model 102R Pioneer 80-ton ballast tractor, GKD 54, helping to unload a Liberation Locomotive at Gladstone Dock, Liverpool. ~ SR

Ernest Holmes

Frederick John Cooper

Preface

When Louise made contact, explaining that her grandfather had been a driver with Edward Box & Co Ltd and had driven the Scammell 100-tonner before asking if I would like to meet him, the opportunity was too good to miss. A meeting was arranged where I also had the pleasure of meeting Mrs Diane Brazier and it quickly became apparent that Fred's career and her father's, Ernest Holmes, were inextricably interwoven. Further meetings were arranged where I was privileged to share their reminiscences and personal archives as the extraordinary story of a lifetime of achievement unfolded. Researching official documents helped provide background and historical accuracy. The emphasis though remains with the personal memories, the kind of history that cannot be found in the record books or documents.

Inevitably, with both Fred and Ernest based at the Birmingham depot of Edward Box & Co Ltd, the majority of information relates to the Birmingham operation, despite Edward Box & Co Ltd being a Liverpool company. Photographs, often just snapshots or many years old, are sometimes not the quality we have come to expect from digital images, but are included because of the atmosphere they portray and story they tell. Much of Fred's heavy haulage work was for the Ministry of Supply during the Second World War and with this work designated secret, no photographs were permitted. Often, Fred, himself had no idea what he was carrying or why.

I am grateful to Louise for making the initial contact and introduction that made this book possible. I am especially grateful to Fred and Diane for allowing me to share their memories and archives and particularly Diane for her hospitality.

My thanks are also due to the staff at the Royal Logistic Corps Museum for their help and access to their archives, to George Baker for his diligent research through the Scammell Lorries Ltd and Pickfords archives. Thanks must also be recorded to the Scammell Register who allowed access to, and use of, their photographic archives. Last but not least, thanks are offered to my wife, Mary, for her continued tolerance of history, especially if it has wheels, and the time spent hidden away on the computer.

Ernest Holmes with his Leyland Subsidy 'A' 3-ton lorry circa 1916 with the company insignia of 62 Coy ASC partly obscured by the canvas cover of the body. ~ DB

The Early Years

Ernest Holmes was born in the Lancashire cotton town of Darwen on 6 June 1897. His parents, Ellen and George, lived at 33 South Street close to the railway station. George worked as a railway carter and Ellen, when Ernest was a small boy, ran a theatrical boarding house. Ernest left school on his thirteenth birthday to work in the cotton mills of Darwen. During the Great War of 1914-18, he volunteered to join the Army Service Corps, enlisting at the Darwen recruiting office on 11 December 1915, some four months before conscription became a reality. He listed his occupation as cotton weaver, but like so many of his contemporaries, the war would change his life beyond recognition.

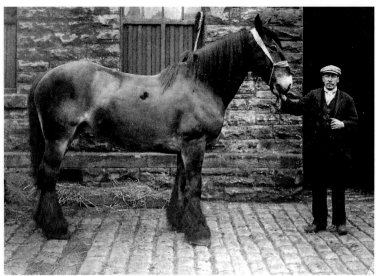

After a period of basic army training, M/20637 Private Ernest Holmes went on to learn to drive a motor lorry and achieve his lifetime ambition. This training would have been undertaken in England and when completed he was attached to 62 Coy (Company) ASC. 62 Coy's role was that of 44 Auxiliary (Steam) Mechanical Transport Coy, which also had a dual role as No.2 GHQ Ammunition Park.

A proud George Holmes poses with his horse while working as a railway carter in Darwen. ~ DB

At the time, 62 Coy, working as No.2 GHQ Ammunition Park, had their headquarters in Arques, a small village 3 kilometres east of St Omer on the N42 Hazebrouck road. St Omer was central to the ASC supply operations to the armies in the defence of Ypres. No.2 GHQ Ammunition Park used a fleet of Commer and Leyland 3-ton petrol lorries and 44 Auxiliary (Steam) Coy a fleet of Foden 5-ton steam lorries.

Ammunition Parks used only petrol lorries. Carrying high explosive shells to the front lines was dangerous enough without the added danger of the fire and resultant sparks from the chimney, needed to provide power to the steam lorry. An additional disadvantage of the steam lorry was the smoke, which made them highly visible and easy targets for the enemy. They were also heavy and caused too much damage to the already badly worn roads. Therefore steam lorries were used mainly further back from the front lines for general transport duties and road building and repair work.

There is no record of 62 Coy prior to 1 September 1915, when they were loading ammunition at the railhead at Arques station and transporting it to Strazeele, St Venant, Lupugnoy and Caestre and also from the ammunition trains to the storage sheds in and around Arques. Driving three tons of high explosive to the front within easy reach and under constant threat of the enemy artillery was arguably the most dangerous work undertaken by any of the ASC companies.

It was also some of the most gruelling as the lorries had to be cleaned and disinfected after every day's work to prevent contamination between the different types of explosives used by different guns. Unusually, ammunition lorries were often fully loaded in both directions.

On 2 February 1916, twelve raw recruits joined 62 Coy to begin their course of 'theoretical and practical instruction in lorry driving' on 3 February. This would have been undertaken at the ASC Mechanical Transport (MT) School of Instruction, based in

Ernest with his parents, Ellen and George and brother, Joe outside their Darwen home. The gentleman on the left is believed to be an actor who was staying at Ellen's boarding house. ~ DB

St Omer. It is conjecture as the recruits are not named and the period from Holmes' enlistment on 11 December 1915 to 2 February 1916 is slightly shorter for basic training than usual. However, there is no further record of new recruits joining 62 Coy and the need for lorry drivers at this time was becoming desperate, so it is conceivable that Ernest Holmes was one of these recruits.

After passing out of the ASC MT School of Instruction, the driver's routine daily life would have been transporting live ammunition or detonators from Arques to the front line. Detonators were never carried on the same lorry as the shells as this was considered too dangerous. The lorries were always run to full capacity with the number of shells carried depending on their weight and size. Ammunition at this period was a rapidly evolving science and often shells or detonators were returned to ammunition parks unused in exchange for newer improved versions. Both outward and return journeys were therefore often undertaken while running at full weight, inevitably adding considerably to the already physically demanding nature of the work.

Ernest Holmes, pictured 3rd from the right in the front row outside Catford Gospel Mission. The ASC had a driver training school at the Catford ASC Depot and Ernest is seen here after passing out of his training before departing to France. After completing their basic training, drivers had their skills honed at ASC MT Schools of Instruction in the locality of whichever company they were attached to. ~ DB

Roads were no more than muddy country tracks as by December 1914 the original pave had been broken up by the heavy traffic and shellfire. The heavily congested narrow roads made passing oncoming convoys difficult and it is unlikely that any driver did not find his lorry ditched at some time. Often the road edge would give way under the weight and the lorry would gently slip sideways into the ditch. A wheel over the edge, even at walking speed meant certain ditching. Ditched lorries were recovered either by others in the convoy, or abandoned to wait for the Mobile Recovery Units to recover them. It all provided extra work for the drivers.

On 15 May 1916 the ammunition park moved to Herlin-le-Sec, three kilometres south of St Pol, some fifty kilometres south of St Omer. From here the company was occupied in collecting ammunition from the railheads at Ligny and Contay and delivering to Rollecourt, Mondicourt, Avesnes in preparation for the Somme offensive due to begin on 1 July 1916. This daily routine continued largely unaltered throughout the Somme battle until 12 October when the company moved to Raincheval and assumed the role of 44 Auxiliary (Steam) Coy.

As an auxiliary company, 62 Coy carried out general transport duties away from the front lines and supported the Royal Engineers with their road repair work. This work was only slightly less arduous, the days still long and road conditions difficult, but at least they were largely away from the stress of the enemy shells. Although headquartered at Raincheval, lorries were sent on detachment to wherever they were needed, to carry out whatever work was needed.

On 14 December the company headquarters moved again to Rubempre a few kilometres to the south, where it remained until 17 April 1917 when it moved to Acheux. It stayed at Acheux until 27 March 1918 when it moved to Talmas on the Amiens to Doullens road. On 8 April the company moved to Hangest on the banks of the River Somme, midway between Amiens and Abbeville, where it remained until 26 September when it moved to Peronne.

The company moved from Peronne to Thy-le-Chateau, fifteen kilometres south of Charleroi in Belgium on 21 November, stopping en-route at Hautmont and arriving at Thy-le-Chateau on 26 November 1918. Here routine work continued in support of the army until 19 May 1919 when it moved to St Saens, 30 kilometres north east of Rouen to continue routine rebuilding work as the company was gradually wound down before returning to England.

62 Coy's records end on 6 June 1919, which is the most likely date they returned to England and the requirement to keep a war diary ceased. Private Holmes remained with the company until demobilised on 29 November 1919. He had learned to drive a petrol lorry, but must have been transferred to the company's Foden steam lorries as his Certificate of Demobilisation shows his 'specialist military qualification' as a 'steam driver'. His place of rejoining in case of emergency was Oswestry.

On demobilisation, Ernest drew £38.5.2d, being the balance he was owed. This sum included the deduction of £1.00.00d for his army Great Coat. Soldiers had the option,

An ammunition park by the roadside on the Western Front. The ammunition would arrive on the Decauville light railway, seen on the left, from a mainline railhead and the motor lorries carried the shells up to the front. ~ RLCM

A Foden 5-ton steam lorry of the type used by 62 Coy ASC. This is the type that Ernest Holmes would have learnt to drive to gain his steam driver qualification. The writing on the body clearly defines it as being used for road work. ~ RLCM

on demobilisation, of either returning their Great Coats or purchasing them for £1.00.00d. Long days in an open lorry during the freezing winters of the Great War convinced Ernest of the value of his Great Coat and he decided they were good value for £1.00.00d, particularly in light of his plans for his life after the war.

The Great War provided the catalyst to transform the road haulage industry in the 1920s. Thousands of men had acquired driving licences with the army and the army had thousands of now surplus vehicles. The huge number of war surplus lorries available determined they were more affordable than before the war. A refurbished 3-ton lorry could be bought in 1920 for one third of the price of a new one in 1914.

After the war, Ernest Holmes bought his own lorry and began his lifetime association with road transport. The first was a steam lorry which he used to carry raw cotton from the docks at Liverpool to the mills of his home town of Darwen. This was soon replaced by an AEC Y-type 3-tonner, which was quite a luxury as it removed the need for the early starts to get steam up before the day's work could begin. It was this lorry that was used to promote Ernest's brother's Angora rabbit business at town carnivals, proclaiming Angora Wool as 'The New British Industry'.

Joe Holmes, Ernest's older brother, who had served in the infantry before becoming a prisoner of war, became an Angora rabbit breeder on his return home. With his wife, Mona, they took the Angora industry to Switzerland and Austria in the 1930s, and presented Benito Mussolini with an Angora wool hat and gloves before returning home to become a world renowned judge and authority on Angoras. He continued to write weekly articles for *Fur and Feather* almost until his death in 1976.

Joe Holmes, 2nd from the left in the front row, in a German prisoner of war camp. The sturdy bar across the outside of the doors and the bars on the window on the right show it is a prison hut and not barracks. The array of different caps suggest some are of German origin. Joe has a 'long service good conduct' stripe on his sleeve which was not issued until 1917. The shiny peak of his cap tells us that it is of civilian and not military origin. ~ DB

Ernest with brother Joe, on the right, enjoy a pipe outside 44 Old Birch. This is where Joe started his rabbitory and where Ernest lived when he married Eleanor Wilson in 1924. Ernest is wearing his ASC uniform which would mean that he had yet to be demobilised, so the year is most likely 1919. ~ DB

Ernest operated out of a garage at 540 Bolton Road, Darwen, close to one of his customers, James Halliwell, who operated 706 looms. It was here that he was to meet his future wife Eleanor Wilson, who ran four of Halliwell's looms. Ernest and Eleanor were married on 24 December 1924 at Belgrave Church, Darwen. A business partnership was also formed between Eleanor's brother, Harold, which was dissolved in 1928 with Ernest taking full control of the business. In addition to the haulage business, Ernest sold petrol, tyres and motor accessories from the garage.

ERNEST HOLMES,
MOTOR TYRES AND ACCESSORIES.
PETROL, OILS AND GREASES.

TELEPHONE 565.
HAULAGE CONTRACTOR.
540 BOLTON ROAD, DARWEN

As well as contracts with the cotton mills, a contract was obtained to transport Ariel motorcycles to the docks for export. This additional work enabled Ernest to purchase a new Leyland SQ2 with a drawbar trailer. The trailer meant a legal obligation for a second driver or trailer mate and presumably this would have been Harold Wilson. The SQ2 was introduced by Leyland in 1926 as a 6/7-ton lorry costing £1060.00.00 with pneumatic tyres and an additional £110.00.00 for the flat platform body. It appears that the AEC was sold to allow for the acquisition of the Leyland.

In the late 1920s, possibly while still operating the Leyland, Ernest joined Marston's Road Services, Lightbody Street, Liverpool. M.R.S., who had a large general haulage fleet, were also one of the leading heavy haulage companies at the time with offices and depots at 117 Borough High Street, London, 27/33 Bell Barn Road, Birmingham and 30 Brazenove Street, Manchester. In 1933, when his daughter, Diane, was born he was sales representative for M.R.S. at their Birmingham office. This was only an office and all the lorries were parked overnight in the surrounding streets.

When M.R.S., by now trading as Edward Box & Co Ltd, moved to Stirling Works, Summer Hill Street, Birmingham, Ernest became the branch manager and by 1939 had become the managing director of the Birmingham branch. By this time Edward Box & Co Ltd had their head office at Speke Hall Road, Liverpool, and had opened further branches in Sheffield, Glasgow and Swansea. Stirling Works was built on a bombed out housing site, the cellars of the houses filled with rubble during the Zeppelin bombing raids of the Great War providing an excellent solid base for the lorries. This remained the Birmingham depot of M.R.S. until nationalisation in 1948.

Ernest Holmes sitting in the driver's seat of his Leyland SQ2 loaded with Ariel motorcycles destined for the Greek Army at the Ariel works in Bournbrook, Birmingham. ~ DB

A wonderful picture of ladies spinning Angora rabbit wool on Ernest's AEC carnival float in the early 1920s. ~ DB

After the war, Ernest joined his brother in establishing a rabbitory before striking out on his own as a road haulier. He subsequently provided his AEC Y-Type lorry as a float to promote Joe's Angora rabbit business in local carnivals. ~ DB

Ernest, on the left and Joe sit proudly with their trophies earned when they were both involved with the rabbit business. ~ DB

Ernest and Joe's prize Angora, Queen of the Isles, *with the Angora Club Challenge Bowl and Fur and Feather Gold Medal won in 1920.* ~ DB

Eleanor Wilson, on the right, in 1917 when she worked as a weaver at James Halliwell, Darwen and ran four looms. Eleanor and Ernest were married on Christmas Eve 1924. ~ DB

Joe's wife, Mona sits contentedly spinning the wool from their Angoras. Mona was an accomplished spinner and weaver and was responsible for the many different products that made the business so successful. ~ DB

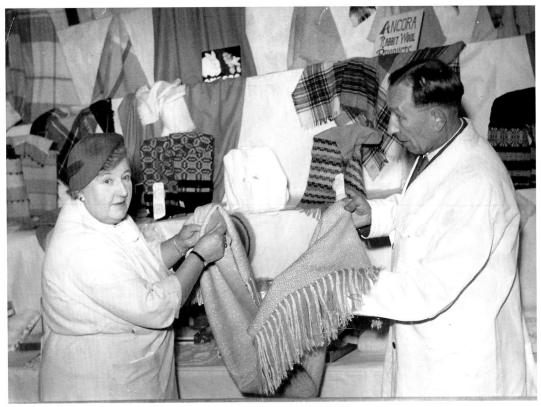

Mona and Joe with the Angora Products display stand at Handsworth Park, Birmingham in September 1957. ~ DB

Ernest's Certificate of Merit awarded by Lancashire & Cheshire Band of Hope & Temperance Union in 1910 for his work done as part of their Scientific Temperance Teaching Scheme. ~ DB

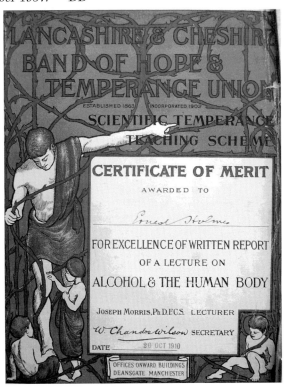

STERN FRAME, WIDTH ON ROAD
18 FEET 4 INCHES. WEIGHT 36 TONS.

M.R.S. Ltd. (formerly Marston's Road Services)
LIGHTBODY STREET, LIVERPOOL,
Depôts at LONDON, BIRMINGHAM, MANCHESTER, LEEDS & GLASGOW.

YU 6307, Scammell SE15 15-tonner, new to M.R.S. in 1927. This eighteen feet wide ship's stern frame weighed thirty-six tons and illustrates both the type of load that earned M.R.S. such an enviable reputation as heavy hauliers and the strength and durability of the Scammell marque. ~ SR

KD 5096, Scammell SE17 25-tonner new to M.R.S. in 1929. This fourteen feet diameter load weighed twenty-six tons and is seen en-route from Wolverhampton to Stockton-on-Tees. John Thompson remained loyal customers of Marston's Road Services and subsequently Edward Box & Co Ltd for many years. ~ SR

KD 9056 with a twenty-five ton shaft bracket for s.s. Mauretania. Note the longer bonnet compared to the previous picture which indicates that the original Scammell petrol engine has been replaced with a Gardner diesel engine. The Scammell radiator badge has been replaced with one that simply states BOX. ~ SR

Some loads needed specialist equipment due to their size rather than weight. Here, KD 9056 with a machinery carrier trailer transports a Ransomes & Rapier 6-ton mobile crane with special extended jib in 1929. ~ SR

SPECIAL VEHICLES FOR HIGH LOADS.

M.R.S. Ltd. (formerly Marston's Road Services)
LIGHTBODY STREET, LIVERPOOL,
Depôts at LONDON, BIRMINGHAM, MANCHESTER, LEEDS & GLASGOW

BOILER SEATINGS.

M.R.S. Ltd. (formerly Marston's Road Services)
LIGHTBODY STREET, LIVERPOOL,
Depôts at LONDON, BIRMINGHAM, MANCHESTER, LEEDS & GLASGOW

M.R.S. employed 'heavy gangs' to install the heavy loads they carried. Here the heavy gang takes a break while installing and commissioning a boiler at an unknown factory. M.R.S. gained an enviable reputation as boiler installation experts. ~ SR

KD 2826 Fowler B6 steam crane, Duke of York, acquired with the purchase of Edward Box & Son Ltd with a 16-wheel, 60-ton trailer and second trailer. The engine carries both M.R.S. and Edward Box livery. ~ SR

Edward Box & Co Ltd
and the One Hundred Tonner

The Edward Box & Co Ltd story can be traced back to the 1870s when William Box was a brickmaker in the Wiltshire town of Market Lavington. William had four sons, William, Edward, Herbert and Alfred. Alfred sought his fortune abroad and William, Edward and Herbert moved the brickmaking business to Liverpool in 1884 to take advantage of the need for bricks at the rapidly expanding Lancashire port town.

As the brickmaking business flourished, Edward moved into his own premises in Brazenose Road, Bootle and divided his time between the brickmaking business and the transport of goods from the growing port of Liverpool. Edward Box & Co soon gained an enviable reputation for the transportation of Lancashire Boilers in particular, and machinery of all shapes and sizes to and from Liverpool's docks for various manufacturers.

Around the turn of the century, Edward Box's son, Norman E Box, moved to South Africa as the agent for Fowler traction engines. When Norman's return was imminent, Edward opened new premises in Ardwick, Manchester. The business was renamed Edward Box & Son in anticipation of Norman joining the family concern. The plan was

BIRMINGHAM

27/33 BELL BARN ROAD.

TELEPHONES :

MIDLAND 1711 (3 LINES).

CONTRACTORS TO H.M. GOVERNMENT.
ON WAR OFFICE AND ADMIRALTY LISTS.

LIVERPOOL.

2 STRAND STREET.

TELEPHONES :

BANK. 8612 & 8613.

A. C.
MARSTON CO LTD

MANCHESTER:

30 BRAZENNOSE ST.

TELEPHONES :

BLACKFRIARS 6054 & 6055.

ROAD TRANSPORT CONTRACTORS.

SHIPPING AND FORWARDING AGENTS.

LONDON:

117 BOROUGH HIGH ST.,
S.E.1.

TELEPHONES :

HOP 2346 (3 LINES).

DAILY SERVICES.

Presented by MR. E. HOLMES

Ernest Holmes' business card. Who A.C. Marston was has proved impossible to ascertain. All known records show Ernest Charles Marston as head of the company. The Birmingham office is top of the list indicating that Holmes had by this time been promoted from salesman to manage the Bell Barn Road depot. It was referred to as the Birmingham depot, but the reality was that it was no more than an office with the surrounding streets used for parking and repairs. ~ DB

Fresh from the factory and seen in Tolpits Lane, Watford at a favourite spot for Scammell to photograph new models and large customer orders. It is logical that this is the first Model Y built, KD 9168, before delivery to M.R.S. Ltd and painting into their livery. ~ RL

that Edward would continue to run the Liverpool business and Norman would run the Manchester business. Norman, however had other ideas and bought his own engine and started what became the famous Norman E Box & Co, heavy haulage specialist.

Edward Box continued heavy haulage in Liverpool, competing with that other great Liverpool heavy haulier, Marston's Road Services Ltd, owned by Ernest Charles Marston. When Edward died in 1925, Norman refused to purchase the business from his widow. That allowed M.R.S. to buy the business and crucially the 'Box' name as Norman E Box & Co had by now built an enviable reputation. Such was the reputation of the 'Box' name, that when Norman sold Norman E Box & Co to Pickfords in 1930, Pickfords attempted through the courts to prevent M.R.S. using the 'Box' name. This proved unsuccessful and M.R.S. was able to use the Edward Box & Co Ltd name until nationalisation in 1949.

Little is known of the origins of Marston's Road Services. The company was started by Ernest Charles Marston in Liverpool, probably, like so many other haulage companies, in the immediate post-war years of the 1920s. The earliest record found for the company is for a second-hand Scammell S12 12-ton articulated lorry, chassis number 937 with carrier 976. The registration number is unknown and it was acquired on 3 September 1925. A further second-hand Scammell S12, registration number KA 933 was acquired on 6 October 1925. The first record of a new vehicle is for a Scammell S12, KA 792 delivered on 21 September 1925.

By the end of the 1920s, M.R.S. had had built up a successful general haulage business, alongside an enviable reputation for the movement of abnormal loads.

The size of the general haulage fleet can be gauged with the addition of twenty-seven AEC 8-wheel rigid lorries between September and November 1933. The list price for these was £1,400.00.00 for the oil engine version, which even allowing for a discount for quantity was a considerable investment when the country was enduring uncertain times. Between 1925 and 1933, a further thirty new Scammells were also added to the fleet and in 1929 the company was sufficiently established to invest in the Scammell Model Y 100-tonner.

Planning the journey of abnormal and overweight loads during the pre-war years was a complex and skilled business. Roads were not as robust as today and were the responsibility of each local authority. Railway and utility companies had yet to be nationalised and each had to be dealt with regionally. The police forces in each area the load was passing through had to be informed and permission to proceed obtained, with or without the need for an escort. Communications were crude, making planning a journey and coordinating the timing of each load with the relevant police a mammoth task. Responsibility for planning at M.R.S. fell to John Towers Robertson who was based at the Liverpool headquarters. He had to survey the route for bridges, power lines, water pipes, drainage pipes, buildings or lampposts and telegraph poles preventing the turning of corners and gradients that would necessitate the service of additional pulling power. With the route surveyed, the complicated task of liaising with all the relevant authorities could begin.

In 1929, M.R.S. were awarded the contract for transporting locomotives made by Todd Kitson & Laird of the Airedale Foundry, Pearson Street, Hunslet, Leeds. These locomotives, built for export and therefore unable to use the rail network due to being of different gauge, required transporting across the arduous and dangerous trans-Pennine routes from Leeds to the docks at Liverpool. In 1929 steam traction engines were the kings of heavy haulage, but Ernest Marston had another idea – to use an internal combustion engine and approached Scammell Lorries Ltd of Watford to build a petrol lorry with one hundred tons carrying capacity.

One of the Todd Kitson & Laird locomotives en-route from Hunslet to Liverpool. The carrier is being run in 65-ton form with additional wheels attached to the front of the bed. By the time this photograph was taken, the trailer-man had been afforded some weather protection. The advertising boards on the cab roof are for Pratts's Motor Oil. ~ SR

Quite where the idea came from is a mystery, but to even think of it at the time shows the measure and forward vision of Ernest Marston. To put the concept of a 100-ton lorry in context, it is useful to glance at the catalogues of the leading lorry manufacturers at the time. In 1929 the AEC catalogue reveals their largest lorry had a payload of 6-tons; Albion 5-tons; Dennis 6-tons; Karrier 12-tons; Leyland 10 tons; Thornycroft 7-tons. Only Scammell, who specialised in articulated lorries, produced anything larger, a 17-ton machinery carrier and the Pioneer intended primarily for military purpose at 25-tons.

Ernest Marston had forged a close relationship with Lt Col Alfred George Scammell and the Scammells in the M.R.S. fleet had a well proven track record. Even so, it must have been an interesting meeting when Marston proposed to Scammell that his company should build a lorry fully four times bigger than anything currently available. It is a measure of Scammell's confidence in the abilities of his Director of Engineering, Percy Garibaldi Hugh and his Chief Designer, Oliver Danson North that Alfred Scammell accepted the challenge. It is impossible to imagine that Marston was not responsible for a great deal of input into the design, considering his wealth of experience with abnormal load transport.

The result was that sales orders 1287, Model Y 100-ton Motive Unit; 1288 100-ton carrier and 1269 65-ton carrier were issued on 23 May 1929. The chassis number of the motive unit was 1428 and the carrier was 1481. The 100-ton and 65-ton carriers were actually the same trailer. The rear bogie design allowed for the addition of a second set of in-line axles to increase the carrying capacity from sixty-five to one hundred tons. An additional pair of wheels was supplied for attaching to the sides

KD 9168. The two sets of wheels on the carrier confirm that it is in 100-ton guise and the rearmost wheels can be seen to be steering the back of the carrier into the factory gateway. The sign on the cab roof states 'It's a Bigger, Better Car on Pratt's Motor Oil'. It would have looked resplendent in its red livery with black shaded white lettering. ~ RL

BLH 21, the second 100-tonner, supplied to H.E. Coley Ltd. Built for the Metallic Ore Production Co Ltd, St Austel, Cornwall, the Garrett stone crusher and carrier remained as one unit for use as a mobile stone crusher to be towed around the Cornish quarries by traction engines. Note the rear steersman's luxurious accommodation. ~ RL

of the carrier bed to spread the load if necessary. When not needed these were stowed under the carrier inside the swan neck.

Scammell always referred to all of their trailers as 'carriers' because articulated vehicles at the time rarely swapped trailers as is commonplace today. Articulation was primarily a means of taking full advantage of the taxation laws at the time. With a remarkable feat of engineering, the first 100-tonner was delivered to M.R.S. on 20 January 1930 and registered in Liverpool as KD 9168. By today's standards, just eight months to design, build and deliver such a vehicle would be unheard of. In fact the time taken was considerably shorter as the 100-tonner took pride of place on the Scammell stand at the Olympia Motor Show held at the end of October 1929.

The cost was a ridiculously small £475.00.00d, the equivalent of £24,300.00 in 2011. In comparison the Scammell Pioneer cost £1992.00.00d in 1929 and £475 would only have bought an Albion 2-tonner or similar. On the same date that the M.R.S. 100-tonner was ordered, sales orders for another Model Y were issued, 1290 and 1291. These were for BLH 21, the second of the two 100-tonners built and delivered to H.E. Coley Ltd on 27 February 1930. The cost was £3100.05.00 for the motive unit and £1800.00.00d for the carrier, a far more realistic total of £4900.05.00, or £251,000 in 2011.

The reasons for the disparity in price have been lost in the mists of time. Maybe Marston financed the building of KD 9168. Maybe it was a deal struck that enabled Scammell to sell BLH 21 to a competitor. Being the only operator of a 100-tonner would have had immeasurable kudos for M.R.S., and the idea had been Ernest Marston's in the first place. Was the original plan for M.R.S. to own both 100-tonners, which would seem logical given that the sales orders were issued on the same day? Without even knowing if it was possible to build such a huge lorry, is it really conceivable that Scammell had another customer in mind from the outset?

Why BLH 21 was ever built remains a mystery. H.E. Coley were agents for various machinery manufacturers and used BLH 21 to transport a Garrett stone crushing machine from Leiston to the Metallic Ore Production Company at St Austel, Cornwall. This was the only job Coley used it for and it was sold immediately afterwards to Pickfords. The journey was completed on trade plates and the lettering on the doors was crudely painted and not at all in keeping with expectation considering the size of the investment. The load itself was well within the compass of steam haulage, indeed, the idea was that the crusher would be kept on the carrier to be moved by traction engine around the Cornish quarries. BLH 21 was certainly no quicker than steam traction, neither was it any cheaper to run. It certainly had impact, but that appears not to have been exploited. Pickfords purchased it, presumably only to prevent M.R.S. acquiring it as it was not until 1934 that BLH 21 was registered, or that a trailer was purchased for it from Crane of Dereham, indicating that they had no work for it.

KD 9168 remained with M.R.S./Edward Box & Co Ltd until nationalisation in 1949 when it passed into the Pickford's fleet. BLH 21 carried just the single load for H.E. Coley and was then sold to Pickfords. Both KD 9168 and BLH 21 continued to work into the mid-1950s before spending a couple of years in retirement before being eventually disposed of in 1957. The availability of war surplus heavy haulers, particularly the Diamond T and Scammell Pioneer and the development of pneumatic tyres capable of increasingly heavy loads signalled the end for the 100-tonners with their solid-tyred trailers that had reigned for a quarter of a century.

The chassis of the 100-tonner was a massive frame constructed of riveted steel plates. Apertures allowed for the fitting of the engine, gearbox and turntable. Power came

KD 9168 carrying a large cylinder from engineering firm Newells from Misterton near Doncaster. The cab, which went through several changes during its life has had accommodation for the crew added but still retains the original vertical windscreen, later changed to a sloping screen. The M.R.S. heritage is clear from the letters mounted on the cab roof. ~ DB

Wherever it went, KD 9168 was bound to draw a crowd of interested spectators, who more often than not soon became a hindrance. Here the crew are preparing to cross the Barton swing bridge while transporting a Nasmyth locomotive from Patricroft to Birkenhead docks for export to either Palestine or India. ~ SR

from Scammell's own 4-cylinder, 7094cc petrol engine rated at 80hp, though this was uprated to 86hp in deference to the gross weight of 130 tons. At just 0.75mpg, it proved too costly to run and in 1932, Pelican Engineering Co (Sales) Ltd of Leeds replaced the original engine with a Gardner 6LW diesel engine producing 105hp and providing a creditable 4mpg.

Scammell's own 4-speed gearbox was used, coupled to a central primary differential using spur gears to double the number of ratios to eight. This transmitted the drive to the two chain wheels connecting the two drive axles. The gear change levers were mounted externally, one each side of the chassis. Changing the sprockets meant slipping the larger sprocket over the smaller one to change the ratio and enable hill climbing. The difference in sprocket size meant that links had to be added or removed from each of the drive chains each time the sprockets were changed.

The drive axles were mounted to the chassis by way of forward mountings on a heavy cross-tube and trailing arms that were ball-jointed to the rear corners. These ball joints allowed each axle to pivot independently and keep all four wheels squarely in contact with the road. The primary differential compensated the two drive axles and the track of the drive wheels on each axle was sufficient to require a further differential in each axle to facilitate turning corners. Rubber buffers were incorporated into the rear of the frame, which made some attempt, at least, to absorb vibration particularly when running empty. With such modest power and great weight, it was inevitable that low gearing would be needed and low ratio first gear was 196:1, enabling gradients of up to 1:10 to be climbed without the help of double-heading with a second motive unit. Top speed in high ratio top gear was 5mph.

Lorries rarely had front wheel brakes at the time and the big Scammell was no exception. Responsible for keeping 130 tons in check down hills were two sixteen-inch internal expanding transmission brakes, mounted one on each of the cross-shafts from the primary differential. These were supplemented by screw brakes on the rear wheels operated by the driver using a wheel. The transmission brakes were operated by either a foot pedal or hand lever. The hand lever permitting re-starts on a gradient without the need for wheel chocks as it left both the driver's feet free for the clutch and accelerator pedals. The wheel operated brakes allowed braking pressure to be set and held constant when descending long hills.

Overheating of the transmission brakes was a constant problem, which brought into play one of the more important roles of the driver's mate. Haulage with motor lorries at the time was a dirty business with lorries usually grimy and oil stained and heavy haulage even more so. The heat from the transmission brake would set fire to the oil and grease and flames would lick the back of the cab. The driver's mate had to jump out and dowse the flames with a bucket of water before they could take hold. A bucket of water was an essential part of the Scammell's in-cab equipment.

The carrier comprised three sections. A massive swan neck connected it to the motive unit through a six inch ball joint and the tremendous strength required came from a three feet diameter cross tube between the side webs. Two steel girders made up the bed and the two in-line rear axles were mounted onto massive rearward projecting trunnions. Sections of railway line were fitted when carrying locomotives, which could be set at the required gauge. A second pair of axles could be added to raise the payload from sixty-five to one hundred tons. The trailer-man was able to steer the second axle by means of a vertical wheel of similar appearance to a ship's wheel. The massive

Boilers for factories and ships were common loads for Edward Box with KD 9168 carrying the largest. A Daniel Adamson & Co Ltd boiler is en-route from Dukinfield, Manchester to an unknown factory in Surrey. The edge of the carrier's steering wheel can be seen to the right of the rear steersman's rather primitive cabin. ~ SR

Working from the Edward Box Glasgow office, KD 9168 is seen transporting a locomotive built by North British Locomotive Co Ltd of Glasgow. This one is bound for Australia. ~ RL

strength of the bed can be gauged from photographs of KD 9168 loaded with locomotives. None show any deflection under the weight of load imposed and an ingot mould made no impression despite weighing sixty-five tons more than the design weight. Over engineering at its finest!

The 100-tonner had been built to service a particular contract. Its sheer size meant that it was suitable for only the heaviest or largest loads and M.R.S. sought to increase its versatility with some developments of their own. Two further beds were built which converted the carrier to three different lengths but still utilised the swan-neck and rear bogies of the original. A bogey was built to attach under the swan-neck to allow the carrier to be used in drawbar form behind either of the steam traction engines still used by M.R.S.

A crew of three was the minimum required, being the driver, his mate and the trailer-man or rear steersman. However, for only the shortest of journeys was the three man crew sufficient. The driver had his work cut out with the heavy steering that required seven full turns from lock to lock. With steering requiring all of a man's strength, sudden corrections in position were out of the question. Positioning had to be precise from the outset, particularly in the confines of towns and cities where the buildings and street furniture often made difficult turns seemingly impossible.

A vital part of the driver's work was to forewarn the rear steersman of upcoming events. With the steersman some eighty feet behind the driver and the noise making shouting instructions impossible, a telecommunications system had to be employed.

Far removed from modern day radios, it was a system of bell rings. A predetermined number of rings would warn the steersman of a left or right hand turn, or when to start braking. The frequently used rapid succession of bell rings meant 'panic stations'. Even at only five miles per hour, 130 tons can soon become an exciting ride with even the slightest gradient. An Alfred Bell Admiralty communication system was tried but found to be too unreliable and the bell system was retained.

The mate was responsible for ensuring that lubrication of the chains and bearings was carried out, refuelling the side-mounted fuel tanks and any other job needed to keep the leviathan moving. A five-gallon bucket of chain oil hung from the chassis and the chains required oiling three times a day. This was done before starting and during the journey. On the road, the mate would jump out and apply oil to the chains with a thick brush while the outfit continued on its journey. With the carrier running on 12-inch wide phosphor-bronze bushes rather than bearings, lubrication kept the mate nearly as busy as the refuelling did. During the winter months the radiator needed draining each night as anti-freeze was not available. Draining failed to completely empty the cooling system and before starting each morning burning rags were used to defrost the water pump while the radiator was being refilled.

The 100-ton trailer behind Fowler B6 traction engine, KD 2826, probably acquired when Ernest Marston bought Edward Box Ltd. The bogie was specially built in-house for towing behind the traction engine and it was fitted with a turntable coupling for the trailer. The two hydraulic screw jacks, operated by large ratchet spanners and used to adjust the ride height of the carrier bed can be clearly seen. It is seen passing through Brecon en-route to South Wales with a sixty-five-ton Fielding press supplied by Shaw's Hydraulic Engineers of Manchester. ~ DB

This tank built by Ruston of Lincoln is being carried on one of the shorter beds that were built to increase the versatility of the 100-tonner. The trailer-man has lost his wheelhouse to accommodate the load and his view of the road ahead made him totally reliant on the driver for instruction. A sign on the carrier proclaims that the vehicle is 'Running on Henley Tyres'. ~ SR

Mounted on the dashboard was a thirty gallon tank which gravity fed the engine. Using a hand pump, it was the mate's job to ensure it was kept topped up from the saddle tanks. The constant vibration slopped the petrol out of the loose fitting cap and the cabin was usually awash with petrol and thick with fumes. When working hard, this combined with the heat and fug-like fumes from the engine to fill the cabin despite the many draughts and holes in the floor. It is testimony to the quality of petrol available that, in the days when smoking bordered on obligatory and the regular backfiring through the carburettor that either of the 100-tonners survived.

Few garages at the time had forecourts able to accommodate the size and weight of the Scammell and electric pumps had yet to be invented. Refuelling had to be done at the roadside with fuel carried from pump to tank in five-gallon cans. Garage staff would disappear when they saw how much handle winding would be needed to fill numerous five-gallon cans, leaving the mate with plenty of hard work. The drivers soon remembered the best garages for filling up and, whether or not it was needed, every opportunity was taken to top up the tanks at these establishments.

The steersman, originally standing on an open platform of the rear of the trailer, but later housed in his steersman's hut, steered the trailer. At his disposal was a three feet diameter steering wheel and a smaller brake wheel. Only the rearward most axle was steerable making the effort needed to steer the trailer immense and often the driver's mate would be despatched to help heave the big wheel round. The brake wheel applied the brakes via a cable and could be set at the required level for long descents. It was commonplace to find the steersman with his feet up and reading a newspaper when his services were not needed.

The world's largest M.G. Cylinder, or 'Yankee Dryer' used for extracting moisture from pulp for paper making. Built by Walmsleys (Bury) Ltd for Albert Reed Ltd it is seen en-route from Bury, Lancashire to Aylesford, Kent. The uneven wear on the rear tyres can be clearly seen, which created a loud thumping sound which alerted everybody to KD 9168's imminent arrival. It is a sign of the times that the crew are all dressed in suits. ~ SR

Edward Box had a second 100-ton trailer built by Crane of Dereham. This trailer was used in drawbar form and it was possible to adjust the ride height and steer each end independently using the hydraulic system. Each bogie ran on eight wheels and the hydraulics were powered by a donkey engine. A surprisingly modern development was the use of air-assisted brakes. Too modern indeed for the Edward Box fleet. Regularly used in conjunction with a Scammell R10 Colonial 60-ton ballast tractor, which had no air compressor, the braking was reduced to the mate turning the hand wheel to apply the handbrake on each bogie. It was used primarily for the carriage of electrical stators and transformers.

The incessant noise and vibration provided every incentive for the crew of KD 9168 to escape at every opportunity. When not filling fuel tanks or oiling chains, the mate would often walk ahead and wait for the Scammell to catch up. The driver and trailer-man would often walk alongside. On long straight sections of road it was not uncommon to find the Scammell, steering and hand throttle set, completely crewless with all three men walking alongside, or even sitting on a grassy bank waiting for it to catch up.

For longer journeys, a complete second crew was utilised. The day crew would begin the journey to a pre-arranged meeting point. The second crew would follow later in a car to rendezvous at the pre-arranged location. Here they would take over the lorry while the day crew went in the car to their digs for the night. The following morning the day crew would take the car to meet the night crew, who would then go to their digs. By leap-frogging each other in this fashion, the big Scammell was kept moving day and night until the journey was completed. Away for days at a time, with scant washing facilities afforded by digs, and no laundry facilities, Edward Box men soon earned a reputation as being some of the dirtiest on the road. This was particularly true of the Liverpool men who learnt not to say who they worked for when booking digs if they were to find a bed.

One of Edward Box's general haulage fleet 25-tonners with a flat trailer accompanied the 100-tonner to carry three-quarters of an inch thick eight feet by six feet steel plates. These were laid down under the wheels when necessary as the heavy weight on solid tyres would soon destroy the road surface if precautions were not taken. Plates were placed directly in front of each of the wheels and a further plate placed in front of it. The lorry was then driven over the first plate and onto the second plate. When the lorry had passed over the first plate, it was lifted and carried into position in front of the second plate, providing a moving conveyor belt of solid road surface. A team of six or eight men were needed to manhandle the heavy plates into position and in this manner the journey was able to continue with weak road surfaces, railway lines and, particularly in towns, water or sewerage pipes protected.

Inevitably progress was slow and the work arduous whenever these plates were needed. When some boiler end plates became available, these were purchased by Edward Box. Being round in shape they could be tipped onto their edges from the trailer and rolled along the road into position which made the work of the crews only slightly less arduous.

One journey up Shap, which had only recently been resurfaced, took over two days as the crew worked tirelessly lifting and moving plates to allow progress. Climbing Shap

Edward Box's second 100-ton trailer built by Cranes of Dereham carrying an electrical stator. It featured hydraulically powered height adjustment on both bogies and modern air-assisted brakes and handbrakes operated by wheels positioned between the bogie wheels. The air-assistance was too modern for Edward Box who had no vehicles with compressors. The solution was to simply ignore the air system and rely on the hand operated brakes. 1932 Scammell R10, GY 1275 is providing the pulling power. ~ DB

had to be done with great care and often on the wrong side of the road as the edges were not strong enough to carry the weight. Likewise, bridges of suspect strength, or known to be weak had to be plated to ensure safe passage. The best bit about Shap was the Jungle cafe. The parking area had a sound base of granite capable of bearing the heaviest of loads and inside the friendly atmosphere and raging fire provided much needed warmth and respite from cold, noisy cabs.

When the wheels had broken through the surface, the 100-tonner had to be jacked up and the plates slid into position under the wheels allowing it to be driven off the plates. The swan neck was joined to the front of the carrier side members by way of 4-inch diameter steel pins, which allowed the swan neck to pivot. Two forged steel hydraulic rams between the swan neck and side members adjusted the swan neck, which in turn lowered or raised the running height of the carrier. The piston for each ram was operated by a large bronze nut which was hand operated using a large adjustable wrench. Extending the length of the rams tilted the swan neck downwards onto the motive unit, which effectively raised the bed of the carrier. Shortening the rams lifted the swan neck against the weight the motive unit and forced the bed to be lowered to reduce the overall running height.

When the motive unit sank into the road surface, it was normal procedure to place wooden blocks under the carrier and then shorten the rams. The carrier would rest on the blocks and unable to lower further, the swan neck would lift the rear of the motive unit to allow steel plates to be positioned under the wheels. If the carrier bogie had broken through the surface, the front of the carrier was raised as far as possible, blocks

KD 9168 passing through Warrington hauling a Beyer Peacock & Co Ltd locomotive from their works in Gorton, Manchester. ~ RL

MILL MOTOR ARMATURE 73 TONS, OFFLOADING AT SITE.

EDWARD BOX & Co. Ltd. (Incorporating M.R.S. Ltd.)
LIGHTBODY STREET, LIVERPOOL.
Depots at LONDON, BIRMINGHAM, MANCHESTER, SHEFFIELD & GLASGOW

A mill motor armature, built by the English Electric Co, Stafford being off-loaded at a new factory for British Guest Keen Baldwins Ltd at Cardiff. A temporary roadway of railway sleepers, topped with steel plates can be seen beneath the wheels. ~ SR

placed under it and then the front was lowered. This caused the carrier to pivot on the blocks which lifted the rear wheels enough to slide steel plates into place.

Bridges over the road caused different problems. When the load was too large to go under the bridge, a different route had to be found, often meaning a diversion of miles down country lanes. Alternatively a temporary roadway had to be built. Every journey with the 100-tonner was guaranteed to provide some obstacle to delay its already snail-like progress.

Tyres generally lasted for about two months before needing replacement. Rarely was the 100-tonner at a depot when new tyres were required. Obtaining the maximum mileage from each set of tyres meant that they usually needed replacement mid-journey. It fell to the crew to remove the wheels which were loaded onto the 'tackle-wagon' and taken to the nearest Scammell agent. In the Birmingham area, the agent was at Tyseley. The agent supplied and fitted the new tyres and the tackle-wagon returned to the waiting 100-tonner. The eight-hundredweight wheels were removed by sliding them on copious amounts of grease daubed onto the roadway. Once the tyres had been renewed the journey could continue, albeit at a slower pace for several miles to 'run-in' the tyres and prevent blow-outs. Small bubbles of air would form in the tyre during the moulding process and if not run-in properly, these would overheat and burst, showering hot molten rubber into the air.

The tyres never wore evenly. By the end of their lives they were a series of flat-spots making them the shape of a thrupenny bit (or 20p piece in today's money). Each flat-spot would thump loudly as the wheel rotated ensuring that whenever the

KD 9168 gets a helping hand from a Foden GHT 50-ton tractor. The mate can been seen giving instructions to the driver as they negotiate a narrow bend on a county road. The different gear ratios of the Foden and Scammell must have made it a difficult combination to drive and it is likely the Foden was only called into help when absolutely necessary. There is no evidence of the Foden in the records that still exist and the writing on the headboard and the style of the fleet numbers is different to Edward Box fleet numbers. It seems likely that it belonged to a local haulier brought in to provide assistance over a short distance. The painted white edges on the wings and headlamp masks on the Foden tell us that it is war time. ~ DB

100-tonner was on the move that the noise would alert everybody of its coming. Passing through towns at night would ensure sleepless nights for the residents, whether they were interested in witnessing the spectacle of such huge loads or not.

The huge weight caused the wheels to slip inside the tyres on the driving axle. This problem was overcome by purchasing the canvas fire hoses that were no longer fit for service from the Liverpool Fire Brigade. These were cut into short strips and placed around the rim of the wheel before the tyre was pressed on. Pressing on the tyres trapped the strips, squeezing them tightly between tyre and wheel. This increased the grip between tyre and wheel sufficiently to prevent the wheels spinning inside the tyre, whatever the weight carried.

Lighting regulations were far more relaxed in the 1930s and the 100-tonner used just two sidelamps, two headlamps and a solitary two-inch diameter rear light. There were no side-markers or reflectors and the lamps were oil, not electric. Electric lighting was tried but electric bulbs were unable to withstand the constant vibration. The rear light was prone to blowing out in the wind or falling off with the vibration. Lanterns around roadworks left by councils were 'borrowed' for when the lorry was parked by the roadside or to replace a lost rear light.

KD 9168's home depot was the M.R.S. yard, by now in Speke Hall Road, Speke, Liverpool, close to where John Lennon Airport now is. All of the Edward Box heavy haulage fleet was kept there, being transferred to the regional depots as and when need arose. It was when based at Birmingham that John William Cooper was a regular driver of KD 9168. John Cooper had worked as one of Edward Box's many sub-contractors in the late 1920s and early 1930s, but with work sporadic during the early 1930s slump he had sold his lorry to become a full-time Edward Box driver.

It was during the late 1930's that John's son, Frederick Thomas Cooper, learnt his trade as mate to his father and, once old enough, by driving one of Edward Box's Bedford 5-ton lorries as a relief driver. Starting work each morning, drivers never knew where they might be that night and often it would be a week, sometimes more before they returned home. Fred lived in Priory Road, Yardley Wood, some five miles from the office. He would get a 5d 'workman's return' bus ticket on the way to work, which he says 'had to come out of my fifty bob a week'. (£2.10.00d or £2.50 in today's money). He would then walk home and use the return ticket to get to work the next day. This enabled him to save enough to buy a *Sun* pushbike for £5.00.00 and save the long walk home after a day's graft. Coincidentally *Sun* pushbikes were made almost next door to the Edward Box depot.

One of Fred's early memories was with his father in a ballast tractor and drawbar trailer descending Mucklows Hill, Halesowen, which in those days was a steep, winding road, not the dual carriageway it is today. Winding on the Neates ratchet brake, the cable snapped with a loud crack which left the trailer with no brakes. Despite the speed of only 4mph, the transmission brake was soon overheating and the

KD 9168 with the 100-ton carrier hauling a Beyer Peacock & Co Ltd locomotive from their works in Gorton, Manchester. The tyres on the rear steering axle can clearly be seen to be nearing the end of their life. ~ RL

disaster of a run-a-way loomed. Fred had to leap from the cab, climb onto the trailer and get one of the 1.5-inch thick iron bars carried as standard equipment. Waiting his moment, Fred thrust this between the spokes of the rear trailer wheels and watched as the bar bent into a neat 'U' shape. It had, however, done its job and the bottom of Mucklows Hill was reached safely.

Fred soon progressed to a Scammell 8-wheel artic which he drove to Rubery Owen at Darlaston and loaded steel fabrications. Back in the yard with the job completed entirely satisfactorily, Fred was told that Head Office had been in contact to state that he was too young to drive the heavy lorries. It was the outbreak of the Second World War before Fred was allowed to drive anything larger than his Bedford again.

Fred's career with Edward Box would go on to last through the war years until nationalisation, when he joined Ernest Holmes in his new venture, Ernest Holmes Ltd. At the tender age of twenty-one, Fred was entrusted with a new 45-ton Scammell and later a Scammell Pioneer, driving some of the biggest loads to be transported in Britain during the war years, a far cry from his first job as an apprentice engine builder upon leaving school.

But, back to Liverpool in 1930 and to the inaugural journey of KD 9168 carrying a load. It was a motor launch built for the Royal Air Force by Harland and Wolff at their works in Bootle. It weighed twenty-five tons, was fifty-six feet long and needed transporting to the Hornby Dock in heart of Liverpool's docklands. Despite the journey of only 1.5 miles, it was a major undertaking at the time and large crowds lined the

PINNACE,
LONDON TO BARROW-IN-FURNESS.

EDWARD BOX & Co. Ltd. (Incorporating M.R.S. Ltd.)
LIGHTBODY STREET, LIVERPOOL.
Depots at LONDON, BIRMINGHAM, MANCHESTER, SHEFFIELD & GLASGOW

Not the Royal Air Force motor launch but a pinnace, or ship's boat, of smaller proportions which was transported from London to Barrow-in-Furness. ~ SR

streets from start to finish to witness the spectacle. The size of the launch dictated that KD 9168 was needed although the relatively low weight meant that the 65-ton trailer was used.

The journey had first been planned on paper to ensure the smooth progress of the job. The launch had been built within a steel frame which was then jacked up using Tangye hydraulic jacks to allow the trailer to be reversed under it. Inside the works, space was very limited with steel frame less than six inches wider than the trailer. Loading took all day and the clearance between the sides of the launch and the walls of the entrance was so small that almost the entire launch had to be through the archway before it could be turned. The roadway was only fifteen yards wide and the wall to a builder's yard opposite had to be demolished. Boiler plates were placed on the ground in the yard to carry the weight and with skilled work by the driver and rear steersman the launch was safely onto the road, ready for the journey to the docks. At the docks the launch was lifted clear of the trailer by the floating crane *Titan* and lowered into the water to start its initial trials.

The heaviest load to be carried by either 100-tonner was an ingot mould weighing 165 tons and with the capacity to accept ingots weighing 200 tons. Manufactured by the Brightside Foundry and Engineering Company of Sheffield it was transported from their Don Road, Newall factory to the Vickers Works of The English Steel Corporation in Brightside Lane, Sheffield on 23 December 1935.

INGOT MOULD 165 TONS

YOU ARE BEHIND THE WORLDS LARGEST LORRY PLEASE DRIVE WITH CAUTION

EDWARD BOX & Co. Ltd. (Incorporating M.R.S. Ltd.)
LIGHTBODY STREET, LIVERPOOL.
Depots at LONDON, BIRMINGHAM, MANCHESTER, SHEFFIELD & GLASGOW

165 tons of ingot mould sits between the girders with its own weight sufficient to prevent it moving. The strength of the carrier is illustrated by the amount of deflection in the girders under the huge weight which was sixty-five tons more than it had been designed to carry. The rear steersman can be seen at his wheel, which must have taken all his strength to turn. It was the heaviest load moved by either KD 9168 or BLH 21. ~ SR

As was often the case, not only with the 100-tonner but with any heavy haulage work, the journey to the job took longer than the job itself. KD 9168 left Liverpool in the morning of Saturday 21 December, arriving in Sheffield at 4.00am on Monday 23. The journey proved more arduous than usual due to heavy snow and ice on the Woodhead Pass and over one ton of salt was used by the crew between Manchester and Penistone to prevent KD 9168 from becoming stranded. Notoriously reluctant to start when cold, five men pulling a rope attached to the starting handle were required to bully KD 9168 into life on the Monday morning.

Loading started at 6.00am following the removal of the factory doors to allow the trailer to be reversed into the factory. Meticulous planning brought together the police, corporation tramway officials and the experienced crew as the difficult manoeuvre from the narrow street through the narrow factory gates was accomplished in front of the gathering crowd. For three hours the normal tram journey was halted, with passengers alighting one side of KD 9168 and continuing their journey on a second tram waiting on the other side. The first attempt at placing the load on the trailer failed when a supporting lug fouled the trailer girders despite the mould being lifted to the fullest extent of the overhead crane. The lifting strops were repositioned and over a dozen men on ropes helped guide the mould onto the trailer for the successful second attempt. Wooden wedges were used to prevent any movement of the mould and its weight meant there was no need for chains or ropes to secure it.

The police cleared the road and the journey began with an escort of corporation and police officials for the one mile journey to the English Steel Corporation's Vickers

EDWARD BOX & Co. Ltd. (Incorporating M.R.S. Ltd.)

SPEKE, LIVERPOOL.

Depots at LONDON, BIRMINGHAM, MANCHESTER, SHEFFIELD & GLASGOW.

TRANSFORMER.
LONDON TO BIRMINGHAM

A transformer being readied for transporting to Birmingham from London. The man on top of the load appears to be securing the tarpaulin sheet. It is running with both rear bogies, indicating that the transformer was too heavy for the 65-ton trailer. ~ SR

EDWARD BOX & Co. Ltd. (Incorporating M.R.S. Ltd.)

A mill motor armature weighing seventy-three tons en-route from the English Electric works at Stafford to British Guest Keen Baldwins Ltd at Cardiff. The mate is standing on the step to gain a better forward view in order to direct the driver and a Road Haulage Association badge can be seen on the radiator. ~ SR

Works. Steel plates were needed to protect tramlines and pipes beneath the road surface and the journey was completed without incident at an average 2mph.

A ninety-eight ton girder, some sixty-eight feet long and ten feet wide proved too large for the world's biggest lorry when it needed transporting from the London North Eastern Railway's goods yard at Marylebone to the Cumberland Palace Hotel being built at Marble Arch in the centre of London.

The movement was made possible with the addition of one of M.R.S. Ltd's fourteen-wheel Eagle trailers. The front of the girder was positioned on a turntable on KD 9168's trailer and the rear of the girder on a turntable on the Eagle trailer. The girder became the means of coupling the two trailers and the turntable on the Eagle trailer was connected to the steering bogie to control the steering of the trailer. The system worked well except on one particularly tight corner when a traction engine was required to winch the steering bogie round to tighten the lock. Built up and ready for the road, the vehicle had six different pivot points. These were the front wheels of KD 9168, the coupling between KD 9168 and its trailer, the rear steering axles of KD 9168's trailer, the front axles of the following Eagle trailer and the two load-carrying turntables.

The journey was completed without incident at 1.5mph, although the number of pivot points did cause the load to gently 'snake' down the road and a truly straight direction was never realised. Forward planning had included building a scale model from Meccano to test the feasibility of the route and chalk marks were used on the road to indicate to the driver the precise route necessary to negotiate the corners. These proved less than successful as the gathering crowds obliterated the marks before the load arrived. The turn from the Marylebone Road into the Edgeware Road proved particularly difficult and required six reversing manoeuvres and some three hours before it was successfully negotiated.

Arguably the most unusual load to be carried by Edward Box & Co Ltd was Eric, a fifty-one ton whale. Purchased by the town of Morecambe, Lancashire for £1,000 and costing a further £1,500 to embalm, Eric was transported from Southend-on-Sea to Morecambe in March 1934. Eric's packing crate overhung the trailer by fifteen feet and Edward Box charged £250 for the journey.

The journey was uneventful except for when, seven days into the trip, the trailer fell through the road surface at the village of Woodseaves, near Eccleshall on the A519. After enlisting the help of two traction engines, Eric was again en-route to Morecambe. Following a civic reception, Eric got stuck at the entrance to the park which was to be home for the rest of the summer season. Five hundred railway sleepers formed the temporary road into the park, but Eric proved too heavy. Eight hours of jacking and pushing followed before Eric could be lifted from KD 9168's trailer and finally took centre stage as Morecambe's star attraction. The empty crate was deposited on oil drums in a field close to Arlewas, near Lichfield where it remained for several months. It is not known what eventually became of it.

Edward Box also had the contract to remove elephant droppings from Dudley Zoo for use as fertiliser. Another unusual Edward Box load was small house, built and presented the Princess Elizabeth in circa 1932, by the people of Wales. En-route to London, behind a steamer, not the 100-tonner, sparks from the steamer's chimney ignited the thatched roof and it had to be returned to Wales for re-thatching.

Eric the whale, purchased by Morecambe Town Council from America as a tourist attraction in 1934. The cab by this time had been extended to provide sleeping accommodation for the crew. The rear overhang of fifteen feet meant that the trailer-man's hut had to be removed although the absence of a rear steersman caused few problems as regulations dictated that major towns had to be traversed at night. ~ SR

During the 1930s, it was the steam locomotives built by Kitsons that kept KD 9168 busy, intermixed with other work. Loads were not always available for such heavyweights as the 100-tonners and they were either left idle or used to supplement the regular heavy haulage fleet in times of need. When transporting the Kitson's locomotives, they were accompanied not only by the lorry carrying the steel reinforcing plates, but also a further 45-tonner. This was to carry the tender for the locomotives which in itself weighed forty-five tons.

Further regular work for KD 9168 was the moving of transformers from the English Electric factories at Stafford and Rugby to the docks at Ellesmere Port. For this a shorter trailer was used. This trailer could be altered by raising the chassis by several feet to create a frame for the transformers to hang in. The shortest of the three available trailer beds was always used for transformers.

Long before the days when driving hours became more regulated and enforced, Edward Box fitted recording devices to their fleet of general haulage and trunk lorries. The forerunner of today's tachograph, they picked up the vibrations of the moving lorry and were used to check that the driver was doing enough work rather than complying with legislation. They were not a permanent fitting and instead were hidden on the chassis of vehicles in a random manner with the driver never knowing whether or not his lorry was so equipped. When drivers found the recorders, they generally destroyed them. It was difficult for management to question the driver too closely about something he should not have known anything about. Drivers can be a canny bunch though and it was commonplace at cafes to see Edward Box trunk lorries with a jack under the rear axle and wheels steadily revolving. The recorder was thereby tricked to show that the lorry was being driven, which kept management happy while the driver enjoyed a hearty meal which kept him happy.

Edward Box & Co Ltd was nationalised on 6 July 1949 and KD 9168 passed into the Pickfords fleet on 1 November 1949, becoming fleet number 6261. Tommy Wolstenholme, a regular driver of KD 9168 in the 1940s joined Pickfords at the same time. It continued to lead a hard working life and was renumbered M350 in October 1956. KD 9168 was finally retired and signed off the Pickfords fleet in October 1957, along with BLH 21. The vehicles from the general haulage fleet were absorbed into British Road Service depots in the areas of the regional offices.

Jack Hardwick of Ewell, Surrey acquired KD 9168 from Pickfords and it languished in a corner of their yard until the late 1960s when restoration was started. Mechanically sound and with new cab it then completed several of the Historic Commercial Vehicle Club's London to Brighton runs for historic commercial vehicles. Jack's grandson, Darren remembers these runs as being quite arduous at 7mph and that Jack was the 'biggest man that you ever did see'. It passed to Maurice Hudson in 1983 and currently resides in the British Commercial Vehicle Museum.

The original 100-ton carrier with the drawbar bogie pulled by Fowler B6, KD 2826, Duke of York en-route from Manchester to South Wales with a Fielding press. ~ SR

Negotiating narrow streets was always a challenge for heavy transport. Disconnecting the bogie from the engine allowed the bogie to be winched round to tighten the steering. The safety chains were essential and one of the Scammell R10 60-ton ballast tractors, probably YY 780, can be seen helping to keep everything under control. Despite the wet weather a small crowd has inevitably gathered and a policeman watches on as the crew slowly inch the load around the corner. These situations always tested the skill of the crews to the limit as reversing back to try again was an option to be used only as a very last resort. ~ SR

The War Years

The outbreak of the Second World War ensured that Edward Box & Co Ltd would be kept busy for the duration of the war, at least. While the 100-tonner was kept busy with locomotives, the Birmingham office held a Ministry of Supply contract for moving tanks built in the West Midlands to wherever in the country they were required. Further Ministry of Supply work included ship's boilers and machine tools for both transportation and storage. The West Midlands' rich engineering tradition provided numerous factories suitable for the Ministry of Supply to commandeer for war work.

Edward Box & Co's great experience with machinery removals made them an ideal choice for the necessary removal of commandeered company's machine tools into storage and the installation of Ministry tools. The drivers were entirely responsible for the safe loading and securing loads and the positioning of the bogies under long loads.

HPP 316 was a 30-ton Tank Transporter supplied to the War Department on 28 September 1944 and used by the American Forces in the UK. It was acquired, with HPP 315, from the Colnbrook Trading Co Ltd who were dealers of war surplus vehicles. Both were registered on 18 May 1946 and used by Edward Box as 80-ton ballast tractors. It became Fred's regular vehicle and is seen negotiating a roundabout in Wolverhampton on the wrong side. Note the condition of the nearside front tyre and the driver's mate, wearing a suit keeping an eye on proceedings mid-way along the load. The column had been loaded at Edwin Danks, Oldbury, who by this time had become part of the Babcock & Wilcox Ltd conglomerate and carries the Babcock name. ~ FC

Edward Box & Co Ltd's premises in Summer Hill Street, Birmingham. ~ DB

A keen and experienced eye was needed to ensure the safety and weight distribution of the load. Edward Box employed teams known as the 'heavy gang' who were responsible for installing or decommissioning the wide variety of loads carried.

Ministry of Supply work was to keep Fred busy throughout the country and despite receiving his call up papers regularly he remained in his 'reserved occupation' throughout. When not moving heavy loads around the country, Fred spent his time volunteering as a despatch rider, although it is difficult working out where he found the time.

Despatch riding meant presenting himself with his own motorcycle at the York Road council depot in Acocks Green. This depot was used for the council's roads department and Fred remembers keeping warm in the engine sheds as the fires in the traction engines were kept in throughout the night. From there he would carry messages to the emergency services and direct them to where they were needed. On one occasion, Fred recalls seeing a double-decker bus blown on its side during a raid on the city centre. Despite the streets full of rubble and conditions making travel next to impossible at times, everybody was determined to continue life as normally as possible.

Among the war time fleet were two Scammell R10 Colonial 60-ton ballast tractors, YY 780 was based at the Manchester depot and GY 1276 at Birmingham. Essentially an export model these were the only two known to have been sold in the UK. Both were supplied new to the Newcastle-upon-Tyne Electric Supply Company with what Scammell described as 'Three Trolley' bodies in 1932. Their purpose was to service remote engineering works by dropping one of the three bodies at each site and then

One of the two Scammell R10s supplied to the Newcastle Electric Supply Company in 1932 illustrates how the Scammell 'Three Trolley' body works. Each body was filled with building materials and left on site and collected when the job was completed. ~ RL

collecting them when the work was completed. This enabled a large number of sites to be serviced by one vehicle, rather than a fleet of vehicles standing at each site while work was in progress. The four driven rear wheels and high ground clearance gave relatively good off-road ability when needed for the more remote sites.

The Colonial was, in Fred's words, 'a bloody awful thing'. With high ground clearance to aid off-road ability for the Colonies, it was a tall lorry. No electric starter meant 'winding it up' with the starting handle, which was at chest level making the swinging particularly arduous. The bronze gears in the central differential were particularly noisy and grated, causing horrendous vibration throughout the whole lorry and any overspeed quickly shattered the gears. Despite the regular oil changes, the oil was always thick with bronze filings. Even by the standards of the day, it was a motor drivers tried to avoid. The only redeeming feature of the Colonial was the excellent winch, which was invaluable to any heavy haulier for loading and positioning loads after unloading. To this day, Fred is grateful that his father was the regular driver of the Birmingham Colonial, leaving him to the more civilised Scammell Pioneer.

The Pioneer cooling system had been designed with the hot climate of the Middle East oilfields in mind, hence the 'coffee-pot' header tank on for the radiator. Large fans on both the Pioneers and 45-tonners drew sufficient air through the radiator that during the winter months they were prone to freezing up, even when running. Sheets of plywood or aluminium were used to blank off the bottom of the radiators in an effort to keep them warm. Cold winter nights meant draining the radiators overnight with the water collected in five-gallon oil drums for refilling the radiators the next morning. Draining the radiators didn't empty the entire system and water pumps were prone to shearing the impellor shaft when frozen. Burning rags soaked in diesel were used to ensure the water pump was thawed out while the radiators were refilled by the mate each morning.

Scammells were notoriously reluctant to get ready for a day's work on frosty winter's mornings. Often passers-by on their way to work were cajoled into giving a pull on the rope attached to the starting handle and it was not uncommon to see four or five burly men bullying the Scammells into life. During the summer months, the drivers competed to determine who was best at holding down the decompression lever while swinging the starting handle single-handed. Once started, of course, they would then run happily all day. It was to the relief of all the drivers when electric starters were fitted to new lorries.

Scammell's Pioneer had an enviable and justified reputation for longevity and ability to just keep on going whatever the conditions. It was also slow, particularly when compared to the American Diamond T. This is clearly demonstrated when hauling a seventy-ton crown for a British Clearing Press from Newcastle-upon-Tyne to Fisher & Ludlow in Castle Bromwich. Fred watched as a Diamond T gradually overhauled him as he struggled up a long gradient until he felt a nudge from behind. His Pioneer picked up speed and even needed a couple of gear changes as his speed gradually increased. Once over the brow, the army Diamond T, complete with tank, pulled out and overtook with the driver giving a cheery wave, which was of course returned by Fred who was grateful for the helping hand.

Access to the factory alongside the River Tyne was impossible for the large heavy haulers. The presses had to be loaded onto a barge and sailed up the Tyne to be

Scammell R10 Colonial, YY 780, registered on 23 September 1932, fleet number 65, was allocated to the Manchester depot of Edward Box. The front bumper is a road spring which cushioned the bumping and banging when it was being used as a pusher. Two of the original Scammell 'trolleys' have been retained as ballast boxes. ~ DB

Fred with his trusty Pioneer, HPP 316, with a Daniel Adamson & Co column for the petro-chemical industry. Note the painted rear number plate and total lack of rear lights. The rear bogie is of Sentinel origin and ran on phosphor-bronze bushes and the front bogie is one built by Gothic Engineering running on Timken roller bearings. The column has been positioned on wooden wedges and just two tensioned wire ropes secure it to each bogie. ~ FC.

transferred to the lorries. Once loaded, with or without the help of a Diamond T, the journey back to Castle Bromwich took 3.5 days. Edward Box only carried a few of these loads with Pickfords doing the bulk of the Fisher Ludlow work.

On another occasion, while en-route to Sheffield, a tiny, flickering light caught Fred's eye in the mirror. Curious as to what it was he watched it for several miles while it gradually caught up his Pioneer as it made steady progress. Eventually, it was alongside and there was a loud knocking on the door. Looking down, Fred saw a policeman on a bicycle who was telling him that he had no rear light. Investigation found that it had blown out and needed no more than a match to execute the repair. With the lamp relit and the policeman happy, the journey was able to continue with the Pioneer resolutely grinding onwards to Sheffield at the speed of a bicycle.

The slow speed of the heavy lorry men created an often more pressing problem. The network of transport cafes provided ample fare for trunk drivers but at the speed of a heavy load, it was hours and not miles that determined the distance from one staging post to the next. A breakdown when en-route to Sheffield meant a long wait for a fitter to arrive from the Liverpool depot. With the nearest cafe miles away, Fred sent his mate into a field to dig a few potatoes which were then roasted on a fire at the side of the road. A hot meal for the crew of a heavy hauler was not always meat and two veg.

Bridges are the bane of the heavy haulier's life. Loads too large to go under or too heavy to go over meant long detours, often using roads unsuitable for heavy traffic. The skew bridge on the A48 en-route to South Wales from the Midlands had no easy

YY 780 carrying a load for Jos Parkes & Son Ltd from Northwich on Sentinel bogies. Nothing is known of this particular load, except that it was a job carried out by the Manchester depot. The drop-well trailer bed has railway-style buffers front and rear indicating that the bogies may have been interchangeable with bogies for operating on the railways. ~ DB

alternative before the Severn Bridge and the M50 motorway were built many years later. On several occasions when carrying ship's boilers to the South Wales ports, Fred found that he had no choice but to unload the boiler from his 45-tonner and drag it on skates or rollers under the bridge before reloading it the other side. To make the task even more difficult as it could only be done at night and in darkness to keep traffic disruption to a minimum.

A bridge en-route to Aberdeen had to be circumnavigated by building a temporary road of railway sleepers across the fields and railway tracks to enable the 100-tonner safe passage. The canal bridge on the A34 north of Talke, Staffordshire entailed a lengthy two hour detour to Knutsford for mobile power stations bound for Old Trafford, Manchester and onward shipment to Russia.

Heavy loads and long or steep hills rarely went together without some degree of clutch slip, particularly with the Scammell 45-tonner. At the top of the long climb past Wigan Pier there was a chemist shop and Fred recalls regularly sending his mate to buy a packet of Fullers Earth for 1d, which was then gently blown into the bellhousing. This stopped any further slip for a while and prevented the clutch from sticking to the flywheel as it cooled.

Never convenient, breakdowns could be a huge problem to heavy hauliers. Trailers were often constructed in-house to suit a particular load or job. Their size meant they could not be simply towed to a workshop or back home. One instance of the disruption caused by a breakdown was on the Chester by-pass. Loaded with a fractionating column from Edwin Danks & Co (Oldbury) Ltd en-route to Birkenhead docks, one of the axles on the trailer bogie broke in two. The trailer had to be left where it was while the axle was removed, taken back to base and a new axle fabricated by an outside contractor. By the time the new axle was fitted and the load able to move again, three weeks had passed. The local council provided oil lamps, more usually found around roadworks, to guard it at night.

Often the load itself comprised the bed of the trailer. Each end of the load was carried on bogies with 'A'-frame drawbars. For particularly long loads, such as fractionating columns for the petrol industry, it was necessary to bolt extensions onto the drawbar. These extensions allowed for longer overhang front and rear, effectively shortening the trailer to negotiate junctions. The downside was that life became more difficult for the driver, who was naturally further away from the fulcrum point and had the problem of huge overhang to contend with. Pushers were often required, not for the weight, but to steer the rear bogie around tight corners. Attendants on foot were required to guide the drivers, keeping a watchful eye on both front and rear to keep the ends of the load clear of vulnerable street furniture. Extensions front and rear severely tested the skills of the drivers and attendants and raised the art of teamwork to new levels.

By the end of the 1930s, the days of the steam lorry were all but finished except in a few specialised operations. Sentinels increasingly consigned to the scrap yard proved a ready supply of axles for heavy haulage bogies. The double drive rear bogies of the 6 and 8-wheel Sentinels proved admirably suited for conversion to heavy haulage

GKC 867, with Sentinel bogies with extensions carrying a fractionating column made by Babcock & Wilcox for E.B. Badger & Sons, destined for the Anglo-Persian oil refinery at Abadan, Iran. The offside bonnet side has been removed to aid cooling and the crumpled front wing and painted out M.O.T. numbers give fleet number 159 a rather weather-beaten look. The driver's mate took great pride in keeping the pipework under the bonnet highly polished. ~ DB

bogies. Edward Box's original bogies ran on phosphor-bronze bushes which required almost constant greasing, although later ones used Timken roller bearings. The bushes caused a build up of static electricity which would give a nasty shock to anybody touching the load. It quickly became normal practice to throw a chain over the bogie and let it touch the ground to earth the load before unchaining could begin. Bogies were more commonly referred to as 'camels' by the Edward Box crews and were built by Gothic Engineering Ltd.

Gothic Engineering had been started by Ernest Holmes, and possibly one of the Edward Box directors from Liverpool to convert Sentinel bogies to 'camels'. The factory was originally a large shed with a corrugated steel roof in Hallfords Lane behind the *Hawthorns* football ground in West Bromwich. Gothic later moved to a factory in the centre of West Bromwich full of rusting machinery that Fred remembers having to clear before the move could take place. As the supply of Sentinel bogies began to dry up, Gothic built new bogies from scratch which used Timken roller bearings in place of the Sentinel phosphor bronze bushes.

Regular Ministry work was transporting landing craft, or invasion barges, built by John Thompson Ltd from their works in Wolverhampton to Birkenhead docks. The Scammell 60-ton Colonial Pioneer based at Summer Hill Street was used for the two day journey. On other occasions, Fred's Pioneer, HPP 316 was used. The first day was spent loading and driving to Newcastle-under-Lyme where parking was available on the market square. This was the regular overnight stop for Edward Box drivers, who would find the key to their digs hanging on a piece of string through the letter box. On the second day Birkenhead was reached via Nantwich and Chester. Every effort was made to reach Birkenhead in time to unload on the second day. That meant that it was possible to be back to Thompson's factory to leave the trailer and be home with the tractor unit a day early. Drivers taking their lorries home was common practice during the war as it lessened the risk of the entire fleet being destroyed in event of a bombing raid on the city.

It became a tradition that a member of the John Thompson staff, chosen from either management or the shop floor, would 'launch' each craft out of the factory when it was completed. On one occasion, the stop cock on the bilge pump had been left open, which resulted

Bogie built by Gothic Engineering outside the West Bromwich workshop. Timken bearings were used in place of the phosphor bronze bushes used on the Sentinel derived bogies. ~ DB

An invasion barge built by John Thompson of Wolverhampton en-route for Birkenhead docks. The barge is carried on a flat-bed supported on solid-tyred bogies and the outfit is headed up by a Scammell Colonial 60-ton tractor. ~ FC.

in the craft sinking after it was launched at Birkenhead. A dock crane was needed to lift it back out of the water to be drained and re-launched.

Boilers for frigates were common loads with the destinations organised by the Ministry of War Transport. These could only be loaded with the highest point on the offside of the trailer when travelling north. This was because the bridge on the outskirts of Kendal was lower on one side than the other. Loaded correctly and with the bed of the trailer lowered as far as possible, the bridge could be cleared with only fractions to spare and on the wrong side of the road. Loading the boiler the wrong way meant that the only way under the bridge was in reverse, which of course meant finding somewhere to turn the huge load around on both sides of the bridge.

Inevitably with an organisation the size of the Ministry of War Transport, wires sometimes got crossed. This is particularly so when the pressures of war-time mean that events can quickly overtake the most diligent planning. One such occasion involved a frigate boiler destined for Aberdeen.

After loading at John Thompson, Fred recalls the journey from Wolverhampton to Aberdeen as particularly tedious. This was mainly due to him using a different lorry, while the regular driver, Charlie Fisher was on holiday. This was one of the older 45-ton Scammells with chain drive, which had two sprockets allowing for a change of gear ratios. Top speed on the smaller sprocket was about 7mph. The weight of the boiler necessitated the small sprocket being needed for the entire journey and Fred arrived in Aberdeen two weeks after departing Wolverhampton. On his way home, he

GU 2126 dates from 1929 and is older than the chain-drive Scammell Fred took to Aberdeen with a ship's boiler. The drive chain can be clearly seen and the angle of the lower section shows that the larger sprocket is in use. ~ SR

was diverted into Renfrew for a load at Babcock & Wilcox Ltd. Arriving there, he was asked if he knew how to load a ship's boiler and if he had the right tackle for securing the load. An identical boiler to the one taken to Aberdeen was then loaded – this one destined for Plymouth.

The journey would take it almost past John Thompson's gates in Wolverhampton. Even worse, the Scammell was back on the small sprocket. When Kendal was reached, it was apparent that the boiler had been wrongly loaded and would only pass under the bridge in reverse. Turned around and the bridge negotiated safely, it was then a long reverse into Kendal before a suitable street to turn around again was found. This annoying delay of several hours added to the already slow and tedious journey.

Arriving at Kempsey, just south of Worcester, Fred grew weary of the constant drumming of a tyre that had worn out of shape. Plymouth still seemed an age away, so the depot was telephoned and the tyre problem reported. The tackle waggon arrived to collect the wheel for a new tyre to be pressed on at the Scammell agent in Tyseley. This provided the opportunity for a lift back to the depot, where he found Charlie Fisher and handed him the keys and paperwork. It was Charlie who continued the leisurely journey to Plymouth, while Fred slept in his own bed that night after three weeks spent in digs.

Kendal had a large parking area on the banks of the River Kent in the town centre. The good hard standing and proximity to the town's digs made it popular with the long distance drivers using the A6. It was also favoured the local Ministry man, who could be seen most mornings recording the registration numbers and departure times of the overnighters. One morning a posse of burly drivers confronted him, suggesting that if they saw him again that he might end up in the river. Whether he found a place to hide and collect his numbers is not known but he was never seen on the park again.

Heavy hauliers were always adept at building or modifying trailers to suit any particular need as and when that need arose. Holmes converted the trailer used to carry the invasion barges to pneumatic tyres in 1943. With typical ingenuity, the axles from tank transporters were inverted and fitted in place of the solid-tyred bogies, resulting in a 4-axle, 16-wheel trailer. This was done to carry a large roll of rubber matting from the Southampton area to Farnborough airfield. The forty mile journey took a full day to complete.

At Farnborough it was laid out on the runway and sprayed with water to undergo trials to determine the viability of landing jet fighters on aircraft carriers. Its purpose was to provide a cushioned landing, enabling the jets to dispense with the traditional landing gear in favour of larger fuel tanks. Fred was able to watch the Gloster Meteor land on the rubber strip and with the trial declared a success, the rubber matting was rolled up, reloaded and taken to Portsmouth. At Portsmouth naval dockyard the matting was laid on the deck of *HMS Pretoria Castle* for further testing, although the concept was never used in active service.

HMS Pretoria Castle had been built as a liner by Harland & Wolff for the Union Castle Line. Within months of completion, she was requisitioned and commissioned as an

1944 Scammell 45-tonner GKC 867, fleet number 159, hauls a Babcock & Wilcox column for the petro-chemical industry on Gothic Engineering bogies. The 'A'-frame on the rear bogie is facing forwards suggesting that the load was not sufficiently heavy to need a push from a second tractor. Two chains secure the column to each of the bogies and a third chain supports the 'A'-frame of the rear bogie. A sign on the driver's door states 'M.O.T. 10/Q/3/101' and the small writing below the windscreen states 'Hauliers Ltd'. ~ DB

armed merchant cruiser on 28 November 1939 and used mainly in the South Atlantic. On 16 July 1942 she was purchased by the Royal Navy and converted to an aircraft carrier by Swan Hunter and was commissioned on 29 July 1943. In this guise she was used for trials and as a training ship, never seeing active service before being de-commissioned and sold back to Union Castle Line in March 1946 when she entered service as the *Warwick Castle* after conversion back to a liner.

Important war-time work was delivering and installing the power units to telephone repeater stations. Usually at remote locations, the driver could be sent anywhere between the very top of Scotland to the south coast of England. These consisted of a Lister diesel engine which powered two generators and weighed about eight tons. The value of this work enabled Edward Box & Co to acquire, through the Ministry of Supply, a brand new Bedford OXC tractor unit with a Scammell low-loader trailer when new vehicles were otherwise unobtainable for civilian hauliers. These repeater stations were built by Chance Brothers of Oldbury. Chance Brothers was a leading glass manufacturer and pioneered new technology before the war and made lenses for lighthouses. They had also pioneered the manufacture of cathode ray tubes and the factory was turned over to manufacturing the repeater stations during the war years. In 1945, Pilkington Brothers acquired a fifty per cent stake in the company.

Diane remembers that some of the repeater stations were kept in the loose boxes at the family home since 1937, *Yew Tree*, at Forhill, Kings Norton. These loose boxes were being used to store various manager's furniture and possessions away from the risk of air raids in the city. Diane and her sister, Ruth, earned for themselves 6d per week

One of the power stations for the electrification of Stalingrad en-route to Trafford Park with Scammell Pioneer 80-ton ballast tractor, GKD 56. A Scammell 45-tonner accompanied the power stations with spare sets of axles for the bogies in case of breakdown. These could be changed at the roadside to prevent unnecessary delay to the journey. This load is being carried on a Gothic Engineering bogie at the front and Sentinel bogie at the back. Additional crew would often accompany the convoy in the motor car seen at the rear. ~ RL

1945 Scammell 80-ton Pioneer ballast tractor, GKD 56, fleet number 185. The mobile power station is carried on a Gothic bogie at the front and Sentinel bogie on the rear. It is en-route for Trafford Park, Manchester for onward shipment to Russia. ~ RL

pocket money by keeping the furniture clean and loose boxes free of moths. Strict instructions were issued to the children to never leave doors open, or to ever disclose to anybody what was there.

It was delivering one of these repeater stations that found Fred in the tunnels beneath Dover Castle. Drivers often became installation engineers at the delivery address and installing it in the maze of tunnels and rooms cut into the cliffs below the castle was one week's work and digs had been arranged in the town centre. After the first night it was decided it would be more convenient to stay in the castle and camp beds were arranged in the cookhouse. From here it was possible to look out over the Channel to France and watch the flashes of the German guns close to Calais. Sixty seconds after seeing each flash, the whizz of a shell passing overhead, or a thud of a shell hitting the cliff face would be heard. The Germans provided Fred's entertainment for the rest of the week until the repeater was installed and he returned home for the next one.

The Drakelow Tunnels were a regular destination and always cloaked in secrecy. Deliveries were only permitted at night and the location was a closely guarded secret. Once unloaded, it was not possible to leave until the hours of darkness and special Ministry passes were needed to gain entry to the site. Excavated into the sandstone hills near the village of Kinver, near Kidderminster, the tunnels ran for some 3.5 miles and included workshops and offices. Work on the complex had begun in 1941 and was completed in 1943 and was a secret factory for the Rover car company who were making components for the Bristol Aeroplane Company. Machine tools and power plants were the regular deliveries.

GKD 56, the 'A'-frame on the rear bogie can be seen extending out in readiness for a pusher tractor to be connected if necessary. ~ DB

A contract that was to keep John Thompson Water Tube Boilers Ltd, and therefore Edward Box busy during the war years was the electrification of Stalingrad, now Volgograd, in Russia. The German siege of Stalingrad from 17 July 1942 to 2 February 1943 had left the city almost entirely without power and the battles on the Eastern Front had rendered the Russian power plant makers at Kharkov ineffective. The desperate need for power gave the Russians no option but to seek help from foreign shores and John Thompson supplied seventy-two mobile power plants with the last leaving the factory in Manor Road, Lanesfield, Wolverhampton on 10 December 1945.

These mobile power stations consisted of a boiler capable of using either coal or oil as fuel and a generator with a capacity of 5,000kw and were built onto a flat bed. To transport them to the docks at Old Trafford, bogies were bolted to each end. These bogies were removed at Old Trafford and the bed was loaded aboard ship for Russia. On arrival in Russia, bogies compatible with the Russian railways were bolted on to complete the journey to Stalingrad by rail.

The journey from Wolverhampton to Trafford Park took three days. The first day was spent loading and then the short run up the A34 to the favourite overnight stop at Newcastle-under-Lyme. On the second day, the outskirts of Manchester would be reached with unloading accomplished on the morning of the third day. With the load delivered, the bogies were bolted together for the journey back to the John Thompson works at Wolverhampton. A Scammell 20-tonner with machinery carrier trailer carrying spare bogie axles accompanied the load in case of breakdown.

Regularly, Edward Box drivers would be diverted to the office established in the ship-building yards at Barrow-in-Furness. Here they were engaged in moving sections of submarines from the shed they were built in to the quayside. The Barrow-in-Furness office was purely an administrative office with the vehicles being brought in from other depots as and when the need arose. The Crane 100-ton trailer was used for

Birmingham depot's 60-ton Scammell Colonial, GY 1276, parked outside the depot, with Sentinel bogies bolted together for running home. The gates to Edward Box's yard can be seen above the roof of the parked car on the corner with Nelson Street. Two small cottages adjacent to the yard were converted into offices. ~ DB

these movements and as the trailer negotiated the slope towards the quay, the wheels used to lift clear of the ground, greatly reducing braking control until flatter ground restored all the wheels to terra firma.

One of Fred's more testing journeys was undertaken in April 1948 and earned him fame in the national press. A flash fractionating column built by G.A. Harvey & Co for the Lummas Co (New York) and destined for the Venezuelan oil fields had to be transported from their Woolwich Road, Greenwich works to the Royal Albert Dock on the opposite bank of the River Thames. The ten feet four inches diameter column which was eighty-three feet, eight inches long and weighed 108 tons was carried on two 8-wheel bogies, or camels, and was towed by a Scammell Pioneer, only needing the help of a second Pioneer to push on one particularly steep incline at the start of the journey.

With the bridges on the lower section of the Thames unable to support the weight, and the length making turning some of the corners on London's roads impossible, careful planning was required by the Metropolitan Police, London Transport and the Ministry of Transport. Water Board officials were consulted as to the whereabouts and strength of drains and sewers and at times steel plates were required to protect tramlines. Six weeks of meticulous planning resulted in the journey stretching from the width of the Thames to a tortuous thirty-eight miles that took eighteen hours.

The route took Fred through Kidbrooke, Blackheath, Lewisham, Camberwell and Kennington to cross the river at Lambeth Bridge. Once north of the river the journey

Fred with HPP 316 and eighty-three feet of flash fractionating column about to cross the River Thames via Lambeth Bridge with the Houses of Parliament in the background. The position of the rear bogie clearly shows how far the column had slipped and increased the overhang which was to prove fatal to a set of traffic lights. Two chains attaching the column to each bogie were all that was required to prevent the column rolling off the side. ~ RL

continued past Marble Arch and along the Edgeware Road onto the Marylebone Road and through Kings Cross, Stepney, Poplar and Plaistow to the Royal Albert Dock. Such was the planning that only one set of traffic lights had to be sacrificed to enable the load to negotiate a junction. At one point the load slipped on the rear bogie and one hour was spent jacking it back into position and securing it. The weight distribution had meant that while climbing a hill, the column gradually slipped backwards. Even with a drawbar extension available, the bogie could not go far enough forward under the load otherwise the pusher tractor could not have been attached when required.

Fred firmly believes that had the load not slipped, then the traffic lights would not have been touched. Even after repositioning, the drawbar extension on the rear bogie was too short for the pusher tractor to be able to assist on tight corners.

The column was loaded onto a special cradle built on the deck of the 9,900-ton steamship *Loch Ryan*. This was to enable the column to be rolled off the ship into the sea for unloading when it reached Venezuela. With no heavy lifting or transport equipment available, it was then rolled overland to the oilfield operated by Shell Petroleum Company and into position.

Ruston Bucyrus at Lincoln provided regular loads that were as routine as any heavy or oversize load can be. The excavators, weighing about fifty tons, were not especially heavy or large and were relatively easy for the drivers to chain down. A police escort took care of the route ensuring the smooth, efficient completion of each excavator journey. Abnormal loads, however, always provide plenty of opportunity for life to take a dramatic turn for the worse at a moment's notice.

On one fateful trip an incident further ahead caused the police escort to divert from the normal route. Drivers had to trust the escorts to know the local roads and rural roads that might be considered too small were frequent diversions. Fred dutifully followed his escort down one such road without too much concern until passing a row of cottages, when he felt the trailer slip sideways as the edge of the road collapsed.

The only way to recover the trailer from the once pristine gardens was to unload the excavator and then reload it once the trailer was back on the road. Staff from Ruston Bucyrus were summoned and while awaiting their arrival, Fred used the time to accompany the escort further along the road to see what other problems lay in wait. It was not long before a bridge with a 5-ton weight limit was encountered. With the bridge obviously incapable to withstanding anything like the weight, it took a long reverse to turn round and extricate the load from the diversion and a long wait while the escorts found another more suitable route. It was never discovered what the incident was. Who paid the cost of repairing the gardens is lost with time, but they certainly were not quite so neat after the excavator tracks had done their work.

GKF 11, fleet number 131 is seen leaving the Metro Cammell works at Saltley with a locomotive destined for Argentina. Note the condition of the front offside tyre and the Hauliers Ltd name painted on the scuttle. The M.O.T. numbers on the door have been crudely painted out. ~ DB

One of the train carriages destined for Argentina. Diane is seen second from the left with Ernest's wife, Eleanor alongside and Diane's sister, Ruth fourth from the left. ~ DB

A railway loco and carriages were transported from the Metropolitan Cammell Carriage and Wagon Co works at Saltley, Birmingham to Bristol docks for shipment to Argentina in 1946/7. This work was carried out by Scammell GKF 11 with a swan-neck trailer which Fred collected new from Scammell at Tolpits Lane, Watford. GKF 11 was a 25-ton articulated tractor unit supplied with a low-loader trailer and Scammell's conversion kit to allow its operation as a 45-ton ballast box tractor. The work did not last long and Pickfords took over the contract due to having trailers with pneumatic tyres. Even with the police escort, the relatively light load would usually reach Yate, some twelve miles north of Bristol on the first day, ready for delivery early on the second.

Regular work for GKF 11 was transporting American built ex-army tanks from Hereford to the West Midlands. These weighed thirty tons and a 4-wheel bogie running on 13.50x20 pneumatic tyres was coupled to the front of a 25-ton trailer to increase the capacity to thirty-five tons. To avoid the steepest gradients around the Iron Age British Camp, country roads were taken across to Malvern Link before regaining the main A38 to the Midlands. On one particular journey, it snowed all the way. Fred recalls that climbing hills with the weight was no problem but descending them required first gear and running the tyres along the edge of the road. At the end of a very long drive, he headed straight home, parking the tank outside his house.

It was a tank that was to provide Fred with one of the most exciting, or scary, rides of his career. He had been tasked as second man to Liverpool depot trunk driver, Frank Hayton, to take a tank from the Metropolitan Cammel works in Darlaston to the

Chilwell Royal Army Ordnance Corps depot at Nottingham. Ernest Holmes had designed and made steel channels with wood inserts for the tank tracks to sit on that could be fitted to flatbed trailers. This enabled trunk lorries to be used for carrying tanks if and when required. Scammell 25-tonners were not renowned for their brakes, particularly when loaded with a twenty-five ton tank. All went well, if slowly, until a long down hill gradient. Inevitably as the descent quickened and the efficiency of the brakes declined, the speed continued to increase. With the cab filled with smoke from the transmission brake and with Frank, who was only a little man, gripping the wheel in an attempt to maintain some control, Fred was on the verge of abandoning ship when the hill began to level and the Scammell slowly regained its sedate pace.

Remembered primarily for the heavy haulage side of the business, it should not be forgotten that Edward Box & Co Ltd also operated a large general haulage and trunking fleet. Liverpool, Manchester and Birmingham all conducted general haulage and the lorries were used to supplement the heavy haulage fleet when required, usually with little regard to the overloading laws of the time. Servicing and maintenance of the Birmingham based lorries was done by Beresford, Caddy & Pemberton of Tunstall, Staffordshire.

An integral and important part of the Edward Box business were teams of engineers known as the 'heavy gang'. The heavy gangs were responsible for decommissioning machine tools etc and loading, although the driver was entirely responsible for the positioning and securing the load. The heavy gang were responsible for unloading and

1940 Scammell R6, GKA 634, fleet number 47 based at the Liverpool head office and used for trunking operations. It has the wartime livery of white wing edges and headlamp masks. Being able to buy a new vehicle during the war years was a luxury rarely afforded and needed a Ministry of War Transport licence and is an indication of the importance of Edward Box & Co Ltd to the war effort. ~ RL

installing the plant and machine tools delivered by Edward Box's 'Heavy Section'. The work of the heavy gang was highly skilled and often dangerous work, with machine tools often weighing up to 100 tons and the only equipment available being block and tackle, screw jacks and railway sleepers as packing pieces.

Not all heavy gangs were mobile. Other gangs were permanently based at the customer's premises and, although employed by Edward Box, worked under the direct control of the customer maintaining, commissioning or moving machinery and presses within the factory.

Edward Box & Co Ltd joined a consortium of transport companies to provide a nationwide network of services in 1941. The consortium, Hauliers (Holdings) Ltd had been formed in 1940 and comprised Airlandwater Transport Co Ltd, Beresford, Caddy & Pemberton Ltd, Geo Dickinson & Co (Transporters) Ltd, Eastern General Transport Co Ltd, G.W. Transport Co Ltd, Thackers & Saltergate

The heavy gang take a break from erecting a 5,000-ton press built by The Hydraulic Press Manufacturing Co. The top platen, which weighed 100-tons was raised tier by tier of timber baulks with screw jacks and each new layer built underneath. After raising the platen to the correct height, a second tower was built around the rams of the press and the platen slid sideways into position above the four columns. Once into position, jacking the platen down was simply the reverse of jacking it up. The close tolerances between the columns and the platen meant that extreme care and precision was needed to prevent the platen fouling or damaging the columns. Few people would have been pleased with 100 tons stuck fast twenty feet up in the air and causing thousands of pounds worth of damage at the same time. ~ SR

Transport Ltd and Butterwick & Walker Transport Ltd. Each member company held an equal one hundred Ordinary Shares of £1.00.00d each.

Hauliers Ltd had a combined fleet strength of 321 vehicles and 132 trailers with Edward Box & Co Ltd contributing forty-five vehicles and sixty-three trailers. There were an additional twenty-seven service vehicles and mobile cranes. The group held operating licences totalling 242 'A', eleven 'B', twenty-one 'Contract A', two 'C Hiring' and forty-five 'Defence Permits'. The combined fleet had a total carrying capacity of 4,795 tons and an estimated replacement cost of £657,000.00.00d. The main thrust of the business was general haulage, with warehousing, export packing and furniture removals as ancillary services. Edward Box & Co Ltd provided the mainstay of the heavy haulage service. Ernest Holmes was appointed Birmingham Branch Manager of Hauliers Ltd on 5 January 1949 with a salary of £1,300.00.00 per annum.

The combined size of Hauliers Ltd failed to stave off nationalisation and the inevitable happened in April 1949. The agreement drawn up for the sale of Hauliers Ltd to the British Transport Commission on 6 April 1949 singled out Edward Box & Co Ltd as being the most important operating company. The agreement valued Hauliers Ltd at £875,000.00.00d, which was disputed by the BTC who valued the business at £445,000.00.00d. Hauliers Ltd was put into voluntary liquidation and the dispute over the value continued until September 1954. Although there is no record of the final valuation, it is believed to be £503,000.00.00d. Edward Box & Co Ltd was nationalised on 6 July 1949.

Edward Box's premises in Summer Hill Street were closed and the business and vehicles transferred to the Pickfords depot in Bromyard Lane, Birmingham on 1 November 1949. Ernest Holmes had hoped that he would be made manager of the combined Pickfords/Edward Box fleet but it was the incumbent Pickfords manager who was given the post. This prompted Ernest to leave the organisation, along with several loyal and trusted employees, including Fred Cooper and form his own business, Ernest Holmes Ltd.

During the war, Holmes found himself a regular visitor to the London office, usually taking with him his good friend and manager Fred Barclay. Fred had lost both his legs and by the time he had put on his false legs and struggled to an air raid shelter, the 'all clear' had been sounded. This meant that they would usually wait out any air raids in the office rather than the shelter with Ernest refusing to leave his friend alone. These experiences prompted Ernest to design a wheelchair. This was propelled along by turning handles which drove the chain driven rear axle. Strapped into his chair, Fred was able to rotate and adjust himself and gain a measure of independence. It is thought that the chair was built by Gothic Engineering and when he died it was donated to a local hospital.

Fred with GKF 11 negotiates a particularly tight turn, no doubt with plenty of advice from the crowd. GKF 11 can be seen on the far left at almost right angles to the carriage destined for Argentina. ~ DB

THE GOVERNING DIRECTORS OF

JOHN THOMPSON WATER TUBE BOILERS LIMITED

REQUEST THE PLEASURE OF THE COMPANY OF

Mr. Holmes.

On completion of Contract for 72 Mobile Boiler Units for Russia and the despatch of the last Unit from our works, Manor Road, Lanesfield, near Wolverhampton, at 12.30 and Luncheon afterwards on

MONDAY, DECEMBER 10TH, 1945

A TOUR OF THE WORKS AFTER LUNCHEON WILL BE ARRANGED IF DESIRED.

R.S.V.P. TO:
MR. W. R. EDWARDS
JOHN THOMPSON WATER TUBE BOILERS LTD.
WOLVERHAMPTON

Manchester based bogies borrowed by the Birmingham depot to move this Edwin Danks & Co cylinder. The bogies ran on particularly small wheels and were needed to allow the extra large diameter load to pass under bridges. ~ DB

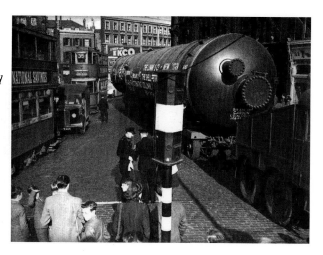

Negotiating the narrow streets of suburbia, Fred misses the buildings and tram No.35 by inches as his journey continues at walking pace.
Two policemen seem to be in earnest discussion while a third keeps a wary eye on the column's passage past the tram. The journey was Fred's epic trip around London to cross the River Thames in 1948. ~ FC

GKC 867, this time with Sentinel bogies carrying a fractionating column made by Babcock & Wilcox for E.B. Badger & Sons, destined for the Anglo-Persian oil refinery at Abadan, Iran. ~ DB

1944 Scammell 45-tonner, GKC 867, fleet number 159 with the police escort reduced to walking speed as a watchful eye is kept on the telegraph pole on the left. The year is 1947 and the front overhang of the fractionating column gives an indication of the length of the 'A'-frame extension in use on the Sentinel bogie. ~ RL

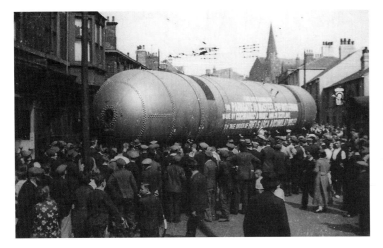

Not much room to manoeuvre this boiler for the Parkgate Iron & Steel Co. of Rotherham with the streets crowded with interested on-lookers. ~ DB

Crowds of spectators make negotiating tight turns all the more difficult as Fred inches his way round the streets of Birmingham with a railway carriage destined for Argentina. ~ DB

Leaving the Saltley works of Metro Cammell, pulled by Fred driving Scammell 45-tonner, GKF 11. Fred had collected GKF 11 new from the Scammell works in Tolpits Lane, Watford as a 25-tonner with a swan-neck machinery carrier trailer. It was converted to a ballast box tractor by Edward Box and used as a 45-tonner. ~ DB

The 110-ton crown of a hammer block being decommissioned by the heavy gang ready for the move from West Bromwich to the Ministry of Supply storage warehouse at Browns Lane, Coventry by Fred using the Crane 100-ton trailer pulled by his Pioneer, HPP 316. ~ DB

TEL.: SME 1695

GOTHIC GARAGE AND ENGINEERING Co., LTD.,

Engineers and

Contractors,

HALFORD LANE, SMETHWICK.

Presented by *E Holmes*

1943 Scammell 54-tonner, GKC 53, fleet number 99 seen at the Manchester depot in war-time livery. ~ RL

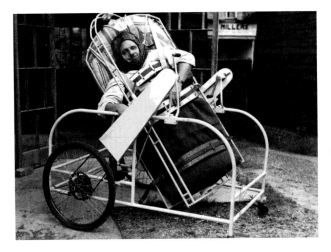

Fred Barclay in the chair designed and built by Ernest Holmes, which could be self-propelled using the side handles. The cradle could also be rotated and raised or lowered without assistance to give his friend back some of the freedom he had lost. ~ DB

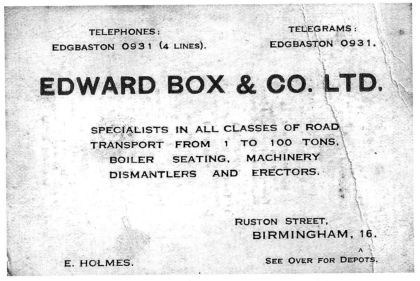

TELEPHONES:
EDGBASTON 0931 (4 LINES).

TELEGRAMS:
EDGBASTON 0931.

EDWARD BOX & CO. LTD.

SPECIALISTS IN ALL CLASSES OF ROAD
TRANSPORT FROM 1 TO 100 TONS,
BOILER SEATING, MACHINERY
DISMANTLERS AND ERECTORS.

RUSTON STREET,
BIRMINGHAM, 16.

E. HOLMES.

SEE OVER FOR DEPOTS.

The Holmes' family home in Cooks Lane, Marston Green from August 1945. Cooks Lane was so named as it led to the hamlet of Bacon's End on the eastern edge of Chelmsley Wood near Solihull. ~ DB

Liberation Locos

The United Nations Relief and Rehabilitation Association had been formed on 9 November 1943 when an agreement was signed by forty-four countries in Washington, USA. Proposed by President Franklin D Roosevelt, its purpose was to help countries rebuild and to repatriate their refugees after liberation from the Axis Powers of Germany, Italy and Japan on the cessation of World War Two. The UNRRA pre-dated the forming of the United Nations and became part of the UN in 1945. In 1947 the UNRRA was dissolved and its work continued under the offices of the World Health Organisation and International Refugee Organisation departments of the United Nations.

In 1946, the Ministry of Supply placed an order on behalf of the UNRRA for 110 locomotives with The Vulcan Foundry Ltd, Newton-le-Willows, Lancashire. They were exported to Yugoslavia, Poland, Czechoslovakia and Luxembourg.

The locos were intended to operate as heavy duty freight trains and the design was a close collaboration between The Vulcan Foundry and the Technical Advisory Committee on Inland Transport (TACIT). The result was a powerful and robust locomotive that embodied the best features of British, American and Continental designs. Built to the standard Berne loading gauge, used in continental Europe they were unable to run on the narrower gauge British railways. The 2-8-0 type locos measured thirty-seven feet eleven inches long, ten feet four inches wide, fourteen feet one inch high and their weight of seventy-five tons ten hundredweights demanded the services of specialist skills and equipment. The tender measured twenty-seven feet seven inches long, ten feet wide, thirteen feet high and weighed twenty-six tons. Transporting the locos from Newton-le-Willows to Gladstone Dock, Liverpool had to be by road and the contract was awarded to Edward Box & Co Ltd.

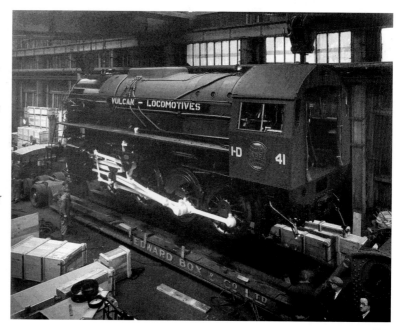

Loading the locos began by positioning the trailer under the two overhead cranes needed to lift the locos in the Vulcan works.

After positioning on the trailer, the loco was jacked up and the spring pins were withdrawn to allow a reduction in the overall height of two inches. ~ SR

After loading the loco onto the 100-tonner, the trailer for the tender was pushed into the loading shed. GKC 294 was a Scammell 45-tonner supplied new in December 1942.

The tender is gently positioned on the trailer using the overhead cranes under the watchful eye of the foreman, while the chap in the cloth cap seems totally unconcerned that twenty-seven tons hangs just above his head. ~ SR

Heavy loads running on solid tyres could be very destructive to road surfaces. To ensure good traction and prevent damage, GKC 294, double-headed KD 9168 through Earlestown and Newton to the East Lancashire Arterial Road before returning to the works to collect the tender.

The fifteen feet six inch railway bridge at Earlestown needed the trailer lowering to within one inch from the road to allow it to be cleared with three quarters of one inch to spare. ~ SR

With Earlestown bridge safely negotiated, the bed of the trailer was raised to its normal running height. Strong muscles were needed to manually raise the seventy ton loco. The crew member leaning against the chassis seems to have picked the best part of the job.

The tight clearance determined that KD 9168 would negotiate the bridge under its own power but once clear, GKC 294 was reconnected to give a helping hand. ~ SR

When the outfit reached the East Lancs Road, KD 9168 was able to continue unassisted along the relatively easy terrain to Liverpool.

GKC 294 was disconnected and returned to the Vulcan works to collect the tender. ~ SR

Positioning the loco and tender on the quay at Gladstone Dock had to be precise. The exact position, or 'set' was marked in chalk in advance.

At the dock, GKC 294 gave way to the extra power of GKD 54, a Scammell 102R Pioneer 60-tonner bought new in March 1945, for manoeuvring in the confines of the busy quay. ~ SR

Once in position the swan-neck was detached from the bed and moved out of the way. The bed was then lowered to the ground. Nothing was easy with only a crow bar and three mates offering more advice than muscle.

The jack in the foreground is one of the four used to lift the loco in order to replace the spring pins that had been removed at the works. ~ SR

Ramps were built to raise the railway lines the eighteen inches from the quay to the trailer bed. Edward Box's steam crane holds the ramp in position while it is packed out with baulks of timber. The swan-neck can be seen behind the locomotive.

The steam crane was used to haul the loco safely down the ramp and onto the rails. ~ SR

The steam crane marshalling the locos and tenders at the dockside to await loading. The ship is the ss Empire Wallace *which loaded the first batch of thirty locomotives with the tenders.*

Lifting the loco from the quayside and lowering it into the hold. Special gear was supplied by UNRRA for uplifting and stowing the locos. ~ SR

'The Gang' at Gladstone Dock
(from left to right)

E. Faulkes ~ Mechanic in charge of off-loading
F. Franco ~ Driver of GKC 294 45-tonner
J. Marshall ~ Driver of KD 9168 100-tonner
E. Briggs ~ Driver of steam crane
W.T. Robertson ~ Road surveyor
L.J. Cope ~ Heavy Section Supervisor
C.J. de Burgh ~ Senior Area Road Haulage Officer, Ministry of Transport
W. Ingham ~ Functional Unit Controller, Heavy Section
A. Ball ~ Erector Foreman, Vulcan Foundry
H. Bramwood ~ Erector Mate, Vulcan Foundry
F. Ball ~ Erector Mate, Vulcan Foundry
F. Heywood ~ KD 9168 Mate

The Ernest Holmes Group

The empire that Ernest Holmes went on to build after Edward Box was nationalised has proved difficult to accurately portray. Fred became managing director of Ernest Holmes (Langley) Ltd and quite naturally his priority was there. His friendship with Ernest and seniority quite naturally gave him an insight into the rest of the Holmes group, but few documents have survived. What is absolutely certain is that it is only possible to offer a glimpse of the scale and diversity of the group, which included road transport, heavy engineering, property management, ore disposal, plant hire, manufacturing, fire salvage and general storage that Ernest built before his death in 1979, aged 83.

The opportunity of managing the Birmingham branch of Pickfords denied him, Ernest Holmes looked forward to a period of relaxation before deciding on his next venture. This opportunity was cut short when he was contacted by the Hardy Spicer company at Tyburn. Hardy Spicer employed one of the Edward Box heavy gangs on a full time contract for maintenance work and expressed a desire to continue working with Holmes, in preference to the gang being nationalised into Pickfords. With the heavy gang also preferring to stay with Holmes, the deal was quickly struck and heavy gangs at other customers throughout the Midlands quickly followed suit.

With regular work and income guaranteed, the new business was established in an office in Ernest's house with the assistance of his long serving secretary, Miss Gladys M. Jaeckel. In addition to the heavy gangs, five enthusiastic and skilled engineering fitters/drivers from Edward Box joined the fledgling undertaking. Ernest remained loyal to these five men, promoting them as new subsidiary companies were added to the group in later years.

Telephone
MARston Green 2580

E. HOLMES

ENGINEER and **CONTRACTOR**

PLANT, MACHINERY & STEEL ERECTOR
FACTORY MAINTENANCE & REMOVALS
COMPLETE INSTALLATIONS, INCLUDING
FOUNDATIONS

CHELMSLEY HOUSE
MARSTON GREEN, Warwickshire

Fred Cooper was one of those young men and with Samuel Layton was one of the original shareholders in the fledgling company. With Layton as managing director of Ernest Holmes (Langley) Ltd, Fred was made the general manager where his great experience with heavy equipment proved an invaluable asset. Sam Layton died in 1954 and Fred became the managing director where he remained until Ernest Holmes (Langley) Ltd became part of the Folkes Group in 1965 where he stayed until his retirement. This promotion brought with it a Jaguar company car in place of his previous company vehicle – an Austin A40 pick-up tackle-wagon. A long line of Jaguars followed and for his fiftieth birthday, Fred treated himself to a Jaguar E-Type.

One of the earliest contracts taken on by Holmes, in addition to the original contracts for his heavy gangs, was the move of Sir William Lyons' Jaguar Cars from Beake Avenue to Browns Lane in Coventry. The post-war success of Jaguar meant

One of Holmes' earliest jobs. An American built press being installed at the Newton Works, Bromsgrove of Garringtons Ltd. The press was transported on its side from Liverpool and required standing up in a pit inside the factory and ancillary parts assembled on it. An ex-RAF David Brown tractor was used to winch the press upright using half-inch cable and snatch blocks. Newton Works had been established in 1940 by Deritend Stamping Ltd as a shadow factory producing stampings for tanks and other military vehicles and was taken over by Garringtons in 1946. ~ FC

that they had outgrown their premises in Beake Avenue and when planning permission was turned down to expand the factory a move became inevitable. The factory in Browns Lane had been a shadow factory for the Daimler Motor Company Ltd, building Merlin aircraft engines during the Second World War and became a Ministry of Supply storage facility post-war. Its size and location made it ideal for Jaguar and tenders were sought in readiness for the move. Various companies that specialised in factory moves were asked to quote, but only Holmes was prepared to offer a fixed price and he was awarded the contract. Despite the agreed fixed price, the final cost was eventually double the original quote as further work was added by Jaguar before the move was completed in November 1952.

Careful planning and an experienced, highly skilled workforce ensured that the move was carried out without a single interruption to production. The different departments within Jaguar were each moved separately outside of Jaguar's normal working hours. Once the final shift on Friday afternoon was finished, the Holmes' team went in action. Heavy gangs decommissioned whichever department was due to be moved and numerous local hauliers were employed to provide transport. The work continued day and night until the department was re-commissioned ready for the opening of the factory gates on the following Monday morning.

The move was the start of a lifelong friendship with Sir William Lyons and loyalty to the Jaguar marque. This loyalty was tested as Holmes' business empire grew and he decided that a new Rolls Royce, purchased from P.J. Evans of John Bright Street, Birmingham, would be more in keeping. His Rolls Royce ownership proved short lived as Eleanor complained that the seats were not as comfortable as she would like. Ernest found himself back at P.J. Evans where he was able to exchange it for his old Jaguar, which had been used in part exchange just a few weeks previously. Doubtless any disappointment with giving up his Rolls Royce was tempered when the part exchange price offered was greater than the price he had originally paid. Rolls Royces had gained a long waiting list as Britain emerged from austerity which created a healthy premium for almost new used cars.

The work of the heavy gangs created a need to provide temporary storage, just had been the situation with Edward Box. Storage facilities, mainly for machine tools, were established at Wellington Street, Winson Green, Birmingham and Stoke Prior Works at Bromsgrove. Although a necessary service, the storage fluctuated and in 1951, the warehouse in Wellington Street was almost empty.

In 1951, Holmes was approached by George Bond and Charles Claffy who were seeking to establish a business to principally cater for the Austin Motor Company's 'completely knocked down' and export traffic. Suitable premises were found at the wartime RAF Station at Childs Ercall near Newport, Shropshire and committed to, when the promised Austin work failed to materialise. This resulted in a vast

ERNEST HOLMES LTD.

Group of Companies

Offer the following Services . . .

LONDON AND THE MIDLANDS

ENGINEERING

Mechanical Hydraulic and Electrical Installations. Factory Removals

Ernest Holmes (London) Ltd.
Murray Street, Camden Town, London, N.W.1
Gulliver 6116/9
Ernest Holmes (Langley) Ltd.
Western Road, Langley Green, Oldbury, Birmingham.
Broadwell 2685/6/7

PLANT HIRE

Cranes, Fork Lift Trucks, Engineering Equipment Low-loading Vehicles

Ernest Holmes (Plant Hire) Ltd.
Worcester Wharf, 14 Bridge Street, Birmingham 1.
Midland 2003 and 2450

TRANSPORT

Daily service to :
London, Liverpool, Manchester, Newcastle Scotland, and South Wales

Ernest Holmes (Transport) Ltd.
Seville Works, Chester Road, Birmingham 24.
Castle Bromwich 3761/2

STORAGE

300,000 sq. ft. of Dry Covered Storage in the Midlands. Cranes and Fork Lifts available

Ernest Holmes (Storage) Ltd.
Seville Works, Chester Road, Birmingham 24.
Castle Bromwich 3764/5

Haulage & Storage

Heavy Haulage to all parts of the British Isles and Continent Covered Storage for : 20,000 Tons Open Storage for : 100,000 Tons

SHROPSHIRE
J. T. Phillips and Son Ltd.
Blest's Hill, Madeley, Shropshire.
Ironbridge 2128

1954 Bedford SA with low-loader trailer loaded with packing cases, possibly for export. It would also have been used for transporting light machinery to be taken into temporary storage, although Holmes only reluctantly operated his own lorries, preferring to use local hauliers when needed. The address on the side is Wellington Street, Birmingham and Ernest Holmes owned a sawmill at Warstock for the production of export packing cases. ~ DB

increase in warehouse facilities when the reality was that less warehousing was actually needed. If disaster was to be avoided, it was crucial that more customers were found. Charles Claffy left the consortium and Holmes and Bond set about building their storage empire.

With dogged persistence and acumen, Holmes and Bond continued to expand the storage business and by 1958 boasted a large and diverse customer base with premises in nineteen locations around the West Midlands. Customers from the motor trade included, British Leyland, Austin Motor Co, Daimler Ltd, Guy Motors Ltd, Jaguar Cars, Morris Commercial Cars Ltd, Rover Cars Ltd, Vauxhall Motors Ltd, GKN Sankey Ltd and Ford Motor Co Ltd. Distington Iron & Steel Co, Garringtons Ltd, Reynolds Rolling Mills Ltd, Loewy Engineering Ltd and High Duty Alloys Ltd provided storage as well as work for the heavy gangs. Diversity was provided by Procter & Gamble Ltd, British Sugar Corporation, Goodyear Tyre Co Ltd, Tate & Lyle Ltd, Berry's Electric Ltd and Boxfoldia Ltd amongst myriad smaller contracts. A contract for the storage of batteries with Chloride Batteries Ltd enabled the Winson Green warehouse to be kept open and eventually filled it to capacity.

The company continued to expand and diversify until 1958 when various subsidiary companies were formed. Faithful to the five men who had joined him at the outset, each was made a director or senior executive of the new companies. These were Ernest Holmes (Langley) Ltd, Ernest Holmes (London) Ltd, Ernest Holmes (Storage) Ltd and later Ernest Holmes (Plant Hire) Ltd and Ernest Holmes (Sales) Ltd. All were formed under the umbrella company of Ernest Holmes Ltd. From beginning just with himself, his secretary and five men, Ernest Holmes employed some 600 men by the time the original company was reorganised in 1958. The Head Office of Ernest Holmes Ltd was at Sheepcote Street, Birmingham.

The years spent at Edward Box had convinced Holmes that he would be better off without the headaches that heavy haulage vehicles brought with them. Consequently he decided that, from the outset, any haulage requirement would be hired in when necessary. Local hauliers were hired for the lighter work and Wrekin Roadways from Telford and Wynns from Newport, South Wales carried the abnormal loads. Vehicles were still needed to carry the heavy gangs and their tackle and the first of these was a Ford ambulance, purchased from a military disposal auction at Measham and converted into a tackle-wagon. The first new vehicles to be acquired were Austin A40 pick-ups in the early 1950s. The expansion of the storage business made lorry ownership more attractive and a Bedford SA articulated unit was acquired with a low-loader trailer in 1954. This began a long allegiance with the Bedford marque.

No opportunity was ignored if there was the prospect of turning a profit and Holmes proved particularly adept at finding a profit in anything he tried his hand at. When

Machines for boring cylinder blocks from the Austin Motor Company in storage at Childs Ercall. They had to be manhandled into position by the heavy gang. J.G. Rose Ltd of Kings Norton, who employed a heavy gang permanently at the Austin works, were responsible for decommissioning the machines and transporting them to Childs Ercall. ~ DB

J.T. Phillips of Madely was taken over their yard contained huge slag heaps. While most would have seen disposing of these as a necessary and expensive cost, Holmes saw the opportunity for profit. The heaps were sold by the ton and there was no shortage of buyers as it was ideal for driveways. With car ownership becoming more available to the masses, everybody wanted the best driveway for their pride and joy.

Many of the new premises taken on for the expanding business were either rented or purchased from Birmingham Corporation. After Holmes had rented from the Corporation their offices in Ouzells Street, Birmingham, the Corporation decided that they needed them back to accommodate the local motor taxation offices. Armed with his contract, Holmes refused to return the offices and instead rented them back to the Corporation. With his characteristic eye for an opportunity, Holmes also won the contract to furnish the offices. It was this deal that opened up the possibilities of further diversifying the business into property management.

When Fisher and Ludlow Ltd moved from their Bradford Street, Birmingham factory to new premises at Castle Bromwich, Holmes took over the factory. Converted to smaller units, it was one of the first such conversions of large industrial premises to small independent industrial units. These units were rented to small companies and later the Head Office was moved from Sheepcote Street to Bradford Street. A large arched gateway between the offices led to the factory and warehousing area to the rear and one of the earliest tenants was the Thorn Electrical Company.

1956 Bedford SA with low-loader trailer of Ernest Holmes (Plant Hire) Ltd. The plant hire business later moved to Berkley Street, Birmingham 1 where it became the Main Dealer and Importer for FIAT OM Fork Lift Trucks. ~ DB

Ernest Holmes (Plant Hire) Ltd, Bridge Street, Birmingham, specialised in the hire of equipment required for heavy machinery removals and the work of heavy gangs providing maintenance services. Forklift trucks of various sizes, industrial trucks and tractors, chain blocks, mobile cranes, pallets and jacks up to one hundred tons capacity were all tools of the trade for the heavy gangs. The hire of these specialised tools dovetailed with Ernest

Shelvoke and Drewry forklift truck, rated at ten tons on the forks and five tons on the hook, outside head office. Part of the Ernest Holmes (Plant Hire) fleet, it spent most of its time in London and was based at the London depot. ~ DB

Holmes (Langley) Ltd, who could provide tools during slack periods or obtain extra tools during busy times, especially 'maintenance fortnight' when the all West Midlands heavy engineering companies scheduled their annual two week holiday for the same dates to accommodate the overhaul of machinery with minimal disruption.

The need for the flexible transport that plant hire required brought Holmes back to heavy lorry ownership with Bedford SA types with low-loader trailers. These were subsequently replaced with Bedford TK tractor units with low-loader trailers. The hire business later led to taking on an agency for the Italian OM brand of forklift trucks.

In 1954, Cedar Homes was formed at Solihull Lodge, High Street, Warstock, Birmingham to manufacture cedar wood bungalows and holiday chalets. These were built to a high standard, using only the best materials and the basic design could be customised to meet individual buyer's requirements. The standard was such that twenty year mortgages were available and at least two of the bungalows are still in use at Fairbourne, Wales. Solihull Lodge was a sawmill owned by Holmes and Cedar Homes complimented the export packing business already established at the mill.

Diane joined the company as the receptionist before quickly proving herself as the general manager. She also took on the responsibility of meeting the building inspectors at new sites and quickly gained their respect in this male dominated profession. She remained at Cedar Homes until 1956 when she left to make the arrangements to emigrate to Australia with John, her husband, in 1957 where John worked in veterinary practise.

She remained in Australia until Christmas 1959 when they returned home with fourteen month old Steven and Christopher expected in June 1960 to establish a veterinary practise in Warwickshire. They bought a run down farm in Weston Lane, Weston-under-Wetherley near Leamington and Ernest provided the necessary materials and skilled labour to build the first purpose built veterinary hospital in

Warwickshire. This could accommodate large and small animals and domestic pets, farm, zoo and even circus animals were treated. As their reputation grew the practise was always full and boasted many celebrities amongst the clientele. Diane remembers that it was not unusual to have an elephant in a field, or even a tiger cub in the living room. The farm outbuildings also provided storage when necessary for Holmes' dealings with fire salvage, which by its nature needed storage at short notice.

A contract to operate a heavy gang maintaining the track and presses at Vauxhall Motors Ltd, Luton, Bedfordshire provided the springboard for Ernest Holmes to establish an office in London. Originally a garage was bought and as the business grew it moved to premises in Murray Street, Camden Town. Further premises were opened in Peckham, although the mainstay of the group remained the West Midlands.

Ernest Holmes (Langley) Ltd remained faithful to origins of the business before being taken over by John Folkes in 1965. Under the umbrella of Ernest Holmes (Langley) Ltd, it was divided into Ernest Holmes (Pipework) Ltd, responsible for industrial pipe work and Ernest Holmes (Fabrications) Ltd, responsible for the installation and maintenance of heavy machinery and tooling.

The company earned an enviable reputation with both manufacturers and customers of heavy machinery. Often the manufacturer would consult with Holmes when building machinery or plant before arranging transport to the customer and entrusted Holmes entirely with the installation. Plant, such as rolling mills, were usually supplied 'ex-works' and Holmes liaised with manufacturer regarding the order in which different sections should be built and delivered on site to ensure a smooth and successful installation.

When the long established Henry Wiggin & Co Ltd relocated their factory from Wiggin Street, Birmingham 16 to Hereford in the early 1950s, Ernest Holmes won the contract to carry out the move. The heavy gangs dismantled the plant and mills in Birmingham and installed it in Hereford whilst the transport was hired in.

Fred dismissed this rolling mill as being too small to be of any real significance. His Austin A40 pick-up, LVP 683, tackle-wagon gives an indication as to the true size of this rolling mill being installed at the Henry Wiggin factory in Hereford. ~ FC

In addition to the existing plant, five furnaces from GWB Furnaces Ltd were installed to work as one unit to provide the factory with power and heat. These had been transported from GWB's Dudley works by regular contractor, Caudle of Coventry Road, Birmingham. Henry Wiggin manufactured titanium parts for the aircraft industry and Fred recalls their rolling mills as being relatively small in comparison to steel mills.

Liquid storage tanks, while not presenting the challenges of enormous weights, had size and a shape that required skills of a different nature to heavy machine tools. When the Midland Dairy at Wolverhampton needed a tank installed on the dairy's roof, the job was made easier by having the headroom for a mobile crane to be employed. Despite its size, the tank could be lifted with relative ease onto the roof and positioned for fixing and plumbing.

The Midland Dairy at Wolverhamptoon afforded the rare opportunity for the use of a crane. A 25-ton crane mounted on an AEC 6x4 chassis, SUK 584, makes easy work of lifting the tank onto the roof. Wolverhampton based civil engineering and plant hire company, Tarslag, also had depots at Rotherham and Stockton-on-Tees. Tarslag were taken over by Tarmac Ltd in the early 1960s. ~ FC

Few jobs allowed the room to operate a crane and when Courtaulds in Coventry needed a tank moving from the ground floor to the upper floor of their Little Heath factory the same methods learned at Edward Box had to be employed. The tank was moved on skates from the ground floor before lifting to be slid along a steel gantry into the upper floor. The gantry was one of the various sized gantries kept in store ready for use by the heavy gangs as and when required. The tank was lifted by manually raising it on jacks to allow the first tier of a tower to be laid under it. The tank was then lifted again to allow for the second tier of the tower to be laid. Each tier was built from twelve inch square Norwegian timber which, as the tower grew, had to be lifted by block and tackle and manhandled into position. Once at the correct height, the tank could be moved off the tower onto the gantry and winched into the factory.

Norwegian timber was the preferred choice because of its density which meant it did not crush or splinter easily. It was purchased in twenty-five feet lengths and cut into ten to twelve feet lengths for ease of working with. A bonus was paid to the heavy gangs for returning the baulks at the end of each job in an effort to prevent them being abandoned on site. With two men required to swing each baulk onto the lorry, the effort required meant that even the payment of a bonus didn't always ensure the return of the timbers and many were left on site.

Building the tower to raise a tank from the ground floor to upper floor at the Courtaulds factory at Coventry. The heavy gang used block and tackle to lift each of the Norwegian wood blocks used to build the tower as the tank was raised on jacks to be winched through the upper floor wall. ~ FC

No job was regarded as too big. One such example was the installation of a Loewy 12,000-ton hydraulic press at the High Duty Alloys factory in Redditch, Worcestershire. The American built press stood fifty-six feet tall, weighed 800 tons and was inaugurated on 24 February 1953 by Sir Frank Spriggs, chairman of HDA's parent company, Hawker Siddeley Group.

Ernest Holmes (Langley) Ltd decommissioned the press from a Ministry of Supply factory in Wrexham, North Wales. Wrekin Roadways Ltd undertook the transport to the HDA factory, where Ernest Holmes erected and commissioned the press, which was used in the manufacture of aircraft parts. It was one of the few jobs that allowed for the use of a crane. A large gantry crane was used to dismantle the press at Wrexham and was itself dismantled and transported to Redditch for the reassembly.

The scale of the press meant that considerable building work was needed before installation could begin. The hydraulic system was housed in an underground chamber created by excavating 2,500 tons of soil and the foundations required 500 tons of concrete poured in a continuous stream for sixty-seven hours.

With forty-two feet above ground level, the 220 feet long factory roof had to be raised forty-seven feet to eighty-seven feet. During the work to raise the roof, the crane was rebuilt and used to install the press and then dismantled to allow the new roof to be installed over the press.

It required its own electrical sub-station and the four treble-ram pumps were driven by 550hp motors. A 6,500 gallon water tank, two water vessels, twelve air vessels and two large pre-filling tanks also needed installing before the press was operational. Three gas-fired furnaces with ten tons capacity and thirty feet long were required to serve the press with pre-heated billets.

The press comprised two bedplates each weighing fourteen tons. These were anchored with special bolts and set into the foundations as the concrete was poured. The bedplates held the adjustable plates on which the four supporting columns were placed. Each column was forty-five feet long, thirty-one inches in diameter and weighed fifty-three tons. The columns tied the bottom platen to the top platen and guided the crosshead and each one had to be aligned precisely to allow the press to operate. The lower platen comprised three sections with a combined weight of 148 tons. The moving crosshead weighed in total 108 tons and was moved by three hydraulic rams fifteen feet long, four feet diameter and weighing twenty-eight tons operating in cylinders weighing thirty-six tons. The upper platen which completed the press weighed ninety-four tons.

From the HDA sales brochure; the 12,000-tonne Loewy hydraulic press in operation. The massive size of the press is clearly illustrated by the workforce. ~ DB

Some presses provided a seemingly impossible challenge to install. One such press was a 9,600 ton forging press for the English Steel Forge & Engineering Corporation at Sheffield. When the work of installing it was put out to tender, Ernest Holmes was the only company to offer a quotation. The huge frame which weighed 810 tons had to be built horizontally alongside the foundation pit and then lifted upright with the help of the company's overhead crane and Holmes' winches. Once the crane had reached its maximum height, it was disconnected and the rest of the operation completed by winch alone. One winch raised the frame while a second winch was connected to the opposite side to prevent the frame toppling over as it reached the vertical. Once raised to the vertical, the frame had to be manually jacked into position in the foundation pit. Six men were employed assembling the frame, with a further two men brought in to assist with the lift and the work took six months to complete.

On 24 March 1965, Ernest Holmes (Langley) Ltd and Ernest Holmes (Plant Hire) Ltd were sold to the John Folkes HEFO group for £123,749.15.00, the equivalent of 5.2 million pounds in economic value in 2011. Fred remained as managing director within the HEFO group until his retirement.

The final stages of erecting the main frame unit of a 9,600-ton forging press for the English Steel Forge & Engineering Corporation at Sheffield. ~ FC

Probably the biggest contracts that Fred worked on, or oversaw, were the installation of rolling mills at the Brtish Steel Corporation's Consett and Scunthorpe steel works. The vast mills were built by Davy United of Sheffield, who were responsible for arranging delivery to site. Once on site, the Ernest Holmes (Langley) Ltd heavy gang comprising thirty men, all highly skilled in their individual trades, had the job of installing and commissioning the plant. From start to finish, close liaison between Davy, Ernest Holmes and British Steel was essential to ensure that the plant was delivered in the right order and at the correct time to allow the installation to be completed as efficiently as possible. Not for the first time, Ernest Holmes (Langley) Ltd won these contracts because they were considered too big by rival companies, all of whom refused to tender for the work.

Erecting the vast rolling mills at the British Steel Corporation works in Consett. A heavy gang of thirty men with engineering, fabrication, electrical and building skills was required to construct the Davy United built mill. The Adamson Alliance overhead crane has 125-tonne capacity and was used to provide valuable assistance with building up the plant. Fred oversaw the contracts following the take over of Ernest Holmes (Langley) Ltd by HEFO, part of the John Folkes Group. ~ FC

After a long and active life, retirement did not sit easily with Ernest and advancing years had done little to diminish his enthusiasm for new challenges. In 1966, aged seventy, he provided funding and managerial experience by taking a very much hands-on role in Douglas Hardwick's new forklift truck manufacturing company, Henley Forklift Co Ltd. It was originally based at Ashted Works, Bromford Lane, Birmingham before moving to Bradford House, Bradford Street, Birmingham. Holmes subsequently became chairman of the company and Henley Forklifts were to provide what were probably the proudest moments in his long career when the company received the coveted Queen's Award for Industry for export achievement.

Success brought with it a need for larger premises and the company moved to a brand new custom built factory at Blackwood, South Wales. Success and growth continued until 1976 when the company was taken over by Lansing Bagnall Ltd. Ernest Holmes had remained chairman until the take over, when failing health forced his retirement as he entered his eighth decade.

Ernest Holmes full life ended on 29 December 1979, aged 83.

The heavy gang take a break for the photographer while moving the chemical storage tank for Courtaulds, Coventry. In the centre with the almost white shirt is foreman, Jimmy Tristrum with Peter Hart, Frank Kearns and Jimmy Brown behind him. Jack Ellis is wielding the wrench and the gang were all long serving men from the days of Edward Box. ~ FC

Ernest Holmes (Fabrication Division) Ltd, Folkes Road, Lye, near Stourbridge, Worcestershire was formed under the umbrella of Ernest Holmes (Langley) Ltd to maximise the skills and experience gained through years of heavy machinery installations. ~ DB

Not all jobs went according to plan. This Mitchell & Wilkins press weighing some thirty tons slipped from a jack and into the foundation pit, severing a man's arm, while being moved to a new site within the factory at Yate, Gloucestershire for the MAIN Gas Appliances company.

Joe Allen supervised its recovery which took five days to lift out of the pit by hand using screw jacks. ~ FC

Caudle of Coventry Road, Birmingham were regular sub-contractors and are seen here with a 'Powermaster' 21,000 BTU furnace from GWB Furnaces Ltd, Dudley, Worcestershire. Ernest Holmes' heavy gangs were responsible for loading the furnace at GWB and then unloading and installing it at Henry Wiggins Ltd, Hereford. It was one of five furnaces installed to work in combination as a single unit with fully automatic control to provide for the factory's power and heating needs. ~ FC

Building the foundations and erecting the rolling mill at the British Steel Corporation, Scunthorpe. The knowledge and experience gained over the years going back to Edward Box days gave Ernest Holmes (Langley) Ltd the confidence to tender for contracts that others deemed too large to tackle. ~ FC.

Erecting the rolling mill for the extension to the British Steel Corporation at Scunthorpe in 1973. ~ FC

Erecting the Davy United mill at Scunthorpe involved a heavy gang of thirty men and incorporated skills from the construction, electrical, plumbing and engineering trades. ~ FC

1964 Bedford TK of Ernest Holmes
(Plant Hire) Ltd. ~ DB

PLANT: MACHINERY AND STEEL ERECTOR.   STRUCTURAL ENGINEER.
FACTORY MAINTENANCE.   COMPLETE ENGINEERING INSTALLATIONS OR REMOVALS.
MACHINE TOOL STORAGE: BUILDING CONTRACTOR.

ERNEST HOLMES

ENGINEER AND CONTRACTOR

WELLINGTON STREET   HURRO WORKS
WINSON GREEN   STOKE HEATH
BIRMINGHAM 18   BROMSGROVE, Worcs.

E. HOLMES, A.M.Inst.B.E.   Smethwick 0101

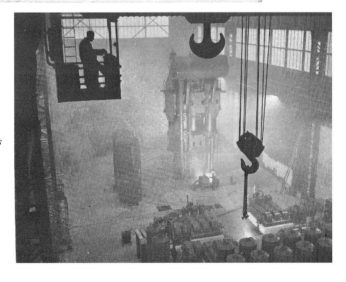

An atmospheric indication of the
size of the 12,000-tonne Loewy
hydraulic press erected in the press
shop of High Duty Alloys Ltd
at Redditch. ~ DB

1960 Bedford SA with low loader trailer loaded with two forklift trucks. Hyster trucks ranging from 2,000lbs to 15,000lbs were the favoured make for the Ernest Holmes (Plant Hire) fleet. ~ DB

Plant, Machinery and
Steel Erector
Structural Engineer
Factory Maintenance
Complete Engineering
Installations and
Removals
Building Contractor
Machine Tool and
General Storage
Specialist
Export Packer and
Manufacturer of
Distinctive
Luxury Chalets

Head Office :
Wellington Street,
Winson Green,
Birmingham, 18.
Telephone : Smethwick 1282/3

Telephone : GULLIVER 7408

ERNEST HOLMES, A.M.Inst.B.E.
ENGINEER AND CONTRACTOR

1 Murray Street,
Camden Town,
London, N.W.1.

Ford Zephyr at the garage in Peckham High Street which became Ernest Holmes' London depot. Diane feels certain that it is Fred stood in the doorway but Fred is not so sure. ~ DB

Diane Holmes at the 1955 Trades Exhibition at Bingley Hall, Birmingham while working for Cedar Homes. She is with celebrity Reg Dixon, who was the tower organist in Blackpool at the time and promoted Cedar Homes at the exhibition. ~ DB

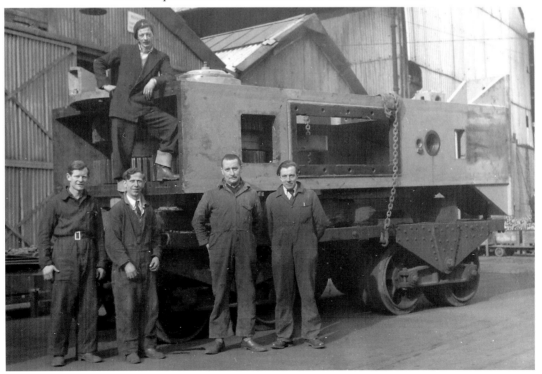

The heavy gang, from left to right, Peter Hart, Skinny Watson (standing on the press), Jimmy Brown, Jack Ellis and Fred Cooper prepare to unload and erect a Mitchells & Wilkins 40-ton press frame at Deritend Stamping, Deritend (Dirty End), Birmingham. ~ FC

Ernest Holmes (left) with Douglas Hardwick and Noelle Gordon, celebrate the opening of Henley Forklift Co Ltd at The Barn, Stratford Road, Hockley Heath. Noelle Gordon star of the television series, Crossroads, and friend of Ernest, had opened the company on 6 January 1966. ~ DB

Ernest Holmes at the handover of the Birmingham Corporation office in Ouzells Street with the Lord Mayor of Birmingham. ~ DB

Ernest Holmes receives the Queen's Award for Industry on behalf of the Henley Forklift Co Ltd in 1973. ~ DB

Ernest Holmes, (3rd from right) listens to a representative of Hill Samuels at the presentation of the Queens's Award for Industry in 1973. The Minister of State, the Welsh Office, Mr David Gibson-Waft presented the award. ~ DB

New Scammells supplied to Marston's Road Services
(vehicles with a trailer number listed were supplied as a complete articulated lorry)

Registration no.	Chassis no.	Trailer no.	Model	Date supplied
KA 792	950	990	S12 - 12-Ton flat trailer	21-9-1925
KA 6812	1079	1131	S12 - 12-Ton flat trailer	11-4-1927
YU 1577	1128		S12 - 12-Ton flat trailer	12-10-1927
YU 2533	1130	1188	S12 - 12-Ton flat trailer	25-10-1927
YU 6307	1131	1183	SE15 - 15-Ton flat trailer	12-12-1927
UC 5319	1154	1211	SE12 - 12-Ton flat trailer	27-1-1928
YV 168	1189	1249	S12 - 12-Ton flat trailer	20-3-1928
KD 903	1151	1196	S12 - 12-Ton flat trailer	26-3-1928
YV 3612	1180	1123	SE15 - 15-Ton flat trailer	2-4-1928
YV 5371	1190	1247	SE15 - 15-Ton flat trailer	7-5-1928
YX 5127	1216	1272	SE15 - 15-Ton flat trailer	13-7-1928
YX 5323	1217		SE17 - 15-Ton flat trailer	1-8-1928
	1252	1279	SE15 - 15-Ton flat trailer	4-10-1928
XV 9186	1264	1315	SE17 - 15-Ton flat trailer	17-10-1928
XV 3098	1255		SE17 - 15-Ton flat trailer	1-11-1928
XV 5337	1259	1337	SE17 - 15-Ton flat trailer	12-11-1928
YX 5667	1276		SE17 - 15-Ton flat trailer	21-11-1928
KD 5096	1274	1336	SE15 - 15-Ton flat trailer	3-12-1928
UL 8251	1325	1381	SE17 - 15-Ton flat trailer	18-3-1929
GU 2126	1336	1392	SE17 - 15-Ton flat trailer	18-3-1929
KD 9168	1337	1393	SE17 - 15-Ton flat trailer	25-3-1929
GP 8438	4128	1481	Y - 100-Ton	20-1-1930
GT 201	1666	1653	15SUP14 LPPNE - 15-Ton*	20-7-1931
GT 944	1667	1654	15SUP14 LPPNE - 15-Ton	5-8-1931
GT 943	1668	1655	15SUP14 LPPNE - 15-Ton	15-9-1931
KF 6881	1669	1656	15SUP14 LPPNE - 15-Ton	16-9-1931
GT 3900 **	1694	1676	15SUP14 LPPNE - 15-Ton	5-10-1931
	1695	1678	15SUP14 LPPNE - 15-Ton	4-12-1931

* SUP LPPNE - Superimposed Trailer (not easily detachable) Low Power Pneumatic Tyre   ** Show exhibit

Appendix ii
New Scammells supplied to Edward Box & Co Ltd

Registration no.	Chassis no.	Trailer no.	Model	Date supplied
EKD 597	2449	2178	15-Ton (LPPNE)	17-9-1938
GKA 633	3243		R6 - 13-Ton 6-wheel rigid	29-5-1940
GKA 634	3244		R6 - 13-Ton 6-wheel rigid	13-6-1940
GKB 841	4438	2375	20-Ton flat trailer	23-12-1941
GKC 53	4621	2651	15-Ton flat trailer	23-7-1942
	4628		R8 - 8-wheel flat body	9-10-1942
GKC 291	4642		15-Ton flat trailer	10-11-1942
GKC 294	1889		45-Ton	3-12-1942
GKB 842	4448	2383	20-Ton flat trailer	23-12-1942
GKC 295	1891		45-Ton	3-2-1943
GKC 536	1905		45-Ton	31-8-1943
	4581		R8 - 8-wheel flat body	22-12-1943
GKC 815	5571		15-Ton	2-7-1944
GKC 770	1927		45-Ton	23-6-1944
GKC 867	1932	1889	45-Ton	3-10-1944
GKC 866	1933		45-Ton	3-10-1944
GKD 54	5750		80-Ton Pioneer	10-3-1945
GKD 56	5751		80-Ton Pioneer	23-3-1945
GKF 11	6046		20-Ton	21-1-1946
GKF 12	6072		20-Ton	22-3-1946
GKF 13	6076		20-Ton	8-4-1946
GKF 16*	6211	1940	20-Ton	29-8-1946
HYB 269*	6228		20-Ton	20-10-1946
HLV 264	6418		20-Ton	3-2-1948
HLV 265	6578		20-Ton	19-2-1948
	6666		R8 - 8-wheel flat body	3-11-1948

* Supplied via Hauliers Ltd.

Vehicles shown with trailer numbers were supplied as matching motive unit/trailer units.

Appendix iii

New AECs supplied to Marston's Road Services

Reg. No.	Chassis No.	Date Supplied	Dealer	Disposed of
	668/248	28-10-1933	Armstrong Whitworth	Hewstone - 27-5-1935
	668/249	7-10-1933	Armstrong Whitworth	
LV 5401	668/250	5-9-1933	Armstrong Whitworth	
	668/251	10-10-1933	Armstrong Whitworth	
LV 5415	668/252	24-10-1933	Armstrong Whitworth	A.H. Newall MOS Q Tpt - 18-4-1940
	668/253	27-9-1933	Oswald Tillotson	
	668/254	27-9-1933	Oswald Tillotson	
	668/255	27-9-1933	Oswald Tillotson	Wilkinson, Bolton onto H.C. Edwards onto scrap
	668/256	7-10-1933	Armstrong Whitworth	J. Thompson, Barnsley onto Onward Transport, Selby
	668/257	20-10-1933	Oswald Tillotson	J.H. Dickinson & Co
	668/258	13-10-1933	Armstrong Whitworth	
	668/259	14-10-1933	Armstrong Whitworth	W. Knowles, Bolton onto T. Mason
	668/260		Oswald Tillotson	Beaumont Bros
LV 5420	668/261	12-10-1933	Armstrong Whitworth	A&H Hardy
	668/262	9-11-1933	Armstrong Whitworth	
LV 5410	668/263	9-11-1933	Armstrong Whitworth	Newstone - 10-7-1936
	668/264	19-11-1933	Armstrong Whitworth	Newstone - 10-7-1936
	668/265	3-11-1933	Armstrong Whitworth	Lee MTC on 31-12-1936 onto Barlow & Phillips
	668/266	3-11-1933	Armstrong Whitworth	J. Thompson onto Knowles onto McBride
LV 5413 *	668/267	20-10-1933	Armstrong Whitworth	Edwards, Brixton onto Seymour Bros.
	668/336	21-6-1934	Oswald Tillotson	Hope Valley Transport
	668/337	21-6-1934	Oswald Tillotson	Risden Semper
	668/338	25-6-1934	Oswald Tillotson	Risden Semper
LV 8540	668/339	21-6-1934	Oswald Tillotson	L. Somerfield onto Dutfield onto BRS, Newport
	668/340	21-6-1934	Oswald Tillotson	Risden Semper
LV 8543	668/341	9-7-1934	Oswald Tillotson	Dutfield onto L. Wakeman onto W. Baldock (24-3-1936) onto F. Webley
	0386/653	Feb. 1942	Edward Box	
* LV 5413	0680/034			Converted to 8-wheels on 28-6-1940 and renumbered 0386/653

Appendix iv

Known second-hand Scammells supplied to Marston's Road Services and Edward Box & Co Ltd

Marston's Road Services

Registration no.	Chassis no.	Trailer no.	Model	First owner	First registered
	937	976	S12 - 12-Ton flat trailer	Morgan	3-6-1925
KA 933	939	978	S12 - 12-Ton chassis only	Morgan	6-10-1925
	983		S12 - 12-Ton flat trailer	Rawcliffe	30-1-1926
RO 7552	1074	1132	SE15 - 15-Ton flat trailer	Hassan (CD+T)	9-6-1927
YU 2361	1139	1198	S12 - 12-Ton flat trailer	Pendell Transport	2-11-1927
YU 2360	1140	1199	S12 - 12-Ton flat trailer	Pendell Transport	7-11-1927
XV 5549	1149		S12 - 12-Ton flat trailer	Hassan (CD+T)	23-1-1928
UL 5907	1329	1385	SE17 - 15-Ton flat trailer	Thackers & Saltergate	1-8-1929

Edward Box & Co Ltd

Registration no.	Chassis no.	Trailer no.	Model	First owner	First Registered
UU 5666	1329	1415	SE17 - 15-Ton flat trailer	A.C. Marston	3-6-1929
UU 5667	1368	1421	SE17 - 15-Ton flat trailer	A.C. Marston	11-6-1929
GY 1275	1758		R10 - Colonial Pioneer	Newcastle Electric Supply Co	5-7-1932
YY 780	1788		R10 - Colonial Pioneer	Newcastle Electric Supply Co	23-9-1932
GT 307	1675		DN12 - 12-Ton boxvan	Fisher Renwick (Plover)	3-9-1937
HPP 316	5582		30-Ton tank transporter	War Department	18-5-1946*
HPP 315	5644		30-Ton tank transporter	War Department	18-5-1946**

* Delivered to War Department on 28-8-1944
** Delivered to War Department on 21-12-1944

Vehicles transferred from Edward Box & Co Ltd to Pickfords on 1-11-1949

Number	No. from 1956	Reg. no.	Chassis no.	First registered	Make & Model	Pickfords depot	Disposed of
M 6247	M 340	GKC 53	4621	15-8-1941	Scammell 20-Ton	Liverpool	3-1957
M 6248		GKC 291	4642	1-12-1942	Scammell 20-Ton		7-1958
M 6249	M 341	GKC 815	5571	25-8-1944	Scammell 20-Ton	Liverpool > Birmingham	3-1959
M 6250	M 342	GKF 12	6072	17-4-1946	Scammell 20-Ton	Liverpool	3-1959
M 6251	M 343	GKF 13	6076	4-1946	Scammell 20-Ton	Manchester	3-1959
M 6252	M 344	GKF 16	6211	11-9-1916	Scammell 20-Ton	Liverpool	12-1959
M 6253		HKB 269	6288	18-10-1946	Scammell 20-Ton	Liverpool	9-8-1954
M 6254	M 345	GAD 869	6240	18-11-1946	Scammell 20-Ton	Liverpool	3-1959
M 6255	M 346	HLV 265	6578	31-3-1948	Scammell 20-Ton	Liverpool	1-1960
M 6256	M 347	GKC 867	1932	16-10-1944	Scammell 45-Ton	Liverpool	7-1958
M 6257	M 348	GKC 770	1927	19-7-1944	Scammell 45-Ton	Liverpool	7-1958
M 6258		GKC 536	1905	6-11-1943	Scammell 45-Ton	Liverpool > Manchester	8-3-1954
M 6259	M 349	GKC 295	1891	6-4-1943	Scammell 45-Ton	Liverpool	7-1958
M 6260		GKC 294	1889	1-3-1943	Scammell 45-Ton	Liverpool	20-9-1959
M 6261	M 350	KD 9168	1428	20-1-1930	Scammell 100-Ton	Liverpool	10-1957
M 6262	M 351	GKD 56	5751	17-4-1945	Scammell 80-Ton	Liverpool	7-1959
M 6263	M 352	HPP 316	5582	17-5-1946	Scammell 80-Ton	Liverpool	4-1957
M 6264	M 353	HPP 315	5664	17-5-1946	Scammell 80-Ton	Liverpool	3-1959
M 6265	M 354	HLV 265	6418	25-2-1948	Scammell 20-Ton	Liverpool	11-1961
M 6266		JKC 414	72516	10-3-1948	Bedford OSS 6/8-Ton	RHE Unit 66/734	8-3-1954
M 6267		GKB 841	4438	5-1-1942	Scammell 15-Ton	Liverpool	26-6-1953
M 6268		GKB 842	4448	1-4-1942	Scammell 20-Ton	Liverpool	28-8-1954
M 6272		GKF 11	6046	6-2-1946	Scammell 20-Ton	Liverpool > Birmingham	21-3-1955
M 6273		GKC 866	1933	11-10-1944	Scammell 45-Ton	Birmingham	13-9-1954
M 6324		GKF 14	14A.1050	14-5-1946	Commer Q3 3/4-Ton	Liverpool	3-1959
M 6325		GKC 585	13068	28-4-1947	Bedford MW 15-Cwt	Manchester	
M 6338		AJD 547	919235	25-11-1942	Fordson Tractor + winch	Liverpool	2-1962
M 6339		GKB 465	664	23-12-1941	IH KR10R Mobile crane	Liverpool	10-1960
M 6340		GKB 466	633	23-12-1941	IH KR10R Mobile crane	Liverpool	10-1960
M 6341		GKB 467	651	23-12-1941	IH KR10R Mobile crane	Liverpool	
M 6389		HUB 812	178200	9-6-1939	Austin 10hp	Liverpool	14-2-1953
M 6390	M 374	KUB 697	81753	22-3-1947	Austin 12hp	Liverpool	5-1957
M 6391	M 375	CKY 343	64836	20-12-1938	Austin 10hp	Glasgow	12-1956

Appendix vi
Hauliers Ltd constituent companies absorbed into British Road Services

Company	Division	Group
Airlandwater Transport Co Ltd	Eastern Division	31H Bishops Stortford
Beresford, Caddy & Pemberton Ltd	North Western Division	14C Stoke
Butterwick & Walker Transport Ltd	North Eastern Division	15D Brighouse
Eastern General Transport Ltd	Eastern Division	32H Kings Lynn
Edward Box & Co Ltd	North Western Division	21C Liverpool
George Dickinson & Co (Transporters) Ltd	North eastern Division	54D Newcastle-upon-Tyne
G.W. Transport Co Ltd	South Eastern Division	33A London E3
Thackers & Saltergate Transport Ltd	Eastern Division	33H Lincoln

KD 9168 carrying one of the Liberation Locomotives from The Vulcan Foundry to Gladstone Dock, Liverpool. The paintwork has lost its original glossy sheen but the Hauliers Ltd name can be seen on the bulkhead. The Ministry of War Transport number 10/Q/3/50 can still be seen behind the passenger door. The Hauliers Ltd companies were originally given AQ numbers on nationalisation prior to receiving their Group Numbers. ~ SR

AQ 1 ~ Hauliers Ltd, Bishop Stortford (Head Office).
AQ 2 ~ Eastern General Transport Ltd, Kings Lynn.
AQ 3 ~ Thackers & Saltergate Ltd, Lincoln.
AQ 4 ~ Beresford, Caddy & Pemberton Ltd, Stoke-on-Trent.
AQ 5 ~ George Dickinson Ltd, Newcastle-upon-Tyne.
AQ 6 ~ G.W. Transport Co Ltd, London E3.
AQ 7 ~ Airlandwater Transport Co Ltd, Bishops Stortford.
AQ 8 ~ Butterwick & Walker Transport Ltd, Brighouse.
AQ 9 ~ Edward Box & Co Ltd, Liverpool.

Appendix vii
Warehouses and offices of Ernest Holmes (Storage) Ltd

In operation during the 1950s

Sheepcote Street, Birmingham 1

* Seville Works, Chester Road, Tyburn, Birmingham 24

* Bridge Street, Birmingham 1

* Scholefield Street, Birmingham 6

Oozells Street, Birmingham 1

Oozells Street Wharf, Birmingham 1

Brasshouse Passage, Birmingham 1

* Deykin Avenue, Birmingham 6

* Wellington Street, Winson Green, Birmingham 18

* Hencage Street, Birmingham 12

Adderley Road, Saltley, Birmingham 8

Hams Hall, Saltley, Birmingham 8

Duddeston Mill Road, Saltley, Birmingham 8

Bradford House, Bradford Street, Birmingham 5

Stone Yard, Deritend, Birmingham 12

Birchall Street, Birmingham 12

Childs Ercall Aerodrome, Newport, Shropshire

* Blest Hill, Madeley, Shropshire

* Iron Bridge, Shropshire

Murray Street, Camden, London, NW1

* Disposed of at end of lease or sold by 1970

Bibliography

Diane Brazier
Personal archives and memories

Fred Cooper
Personal archives and memories

Roy Larkin
Personal archives

George Baker
Pickfords Ltd, Scammell Lorries Ltd, County records

The National Archive
Army Service Corps, Edward Box & Co Ltd, Hauliers Ltd

Royal Logistic Corps Museum
Army Service Corps

The Scammell Register
Photographic archive

The Road Locomotive Society
Manufacturers, County records

Commercial Motor
News and feature articles

Motor Traction/Transport
News and feature articles